So This Is Normal Too?

Deborah Hewitt

Redleaf Press
St. Paul, Minnesota
1995

©1995 Deborah Hewitt

Book design & production: Judy Gilats, *Peregrine Graphics Services*, St. Paul, MN.
Cover photographs by Diane Carter, Paul Woods, and Charles Weber.
Cover painting by Gary Dougherty.

Published by: Redleaf Press
                 a division of Resources for Child Caring
                 450 North Syndicate, Suite 5
                 St. Paul, MN 55104-4125

Distributed by: Gryphon House
                 Mailing address:
                 P.O. Box 207
                 Beltsville, MD 20704-0207

Library of Congress Cataloging-in-Publication Data

Hewitt, Deborah, 1958-
So this is normal too / Deborah Hewitt.
        p.   cm.
     Includes bibliographical references.
     ISBN 1-884834-07-8 (alk. paper)
     1. Child development. 2. Child care. 3. Early childhood education—Parent participation.
     I. Title.
HQ772.H456   1995
305.32'1--dc20

                                                        95-34645
                                                        CIP

Contents

Twelve Ways Parents Can Support Their Provider

1. Make sure your child is well fed and well rested.

2. Drop off and pick up your child on time. If you must be late or absent, call and let your provider know.

3. Say thank you frequently. Show appreciation with a small gift, gift certificate, or flowers. Have your child draw a picture for your provider or make a thank-you note.

4. Read a book to the children for your provider. Share one of your interests, something about your culture, or a talent you possess. Offer to assist on a field trip.

5. If the regulations in your state allow, offer to stay with the children while your provider takes a short break to walk around the block, go to the library, or grocery shop.

6. Treat your provider professionally. Be prompt with payments and considerate of nonworking hours.

7. Adhere to policies. Read information sent home.

8. Arrange a backup plan for when your child is sick or your provider needs time off.

9. Allow adequate time at drop-off and pickup for your child to make the transition from one caregiver to another.

10. Appreciate that your provider is caring for a group of children.

11. Share information that will assist your provider in caring for your child (for example, a parent being out of town for an extended period or the results of developmental screening).

12. Communicate early about concerns, before resentment builds.

Twelve Ways Providers Can Support Parents

1. Do everything possible to keep children safe and well cared for.

2. Make it fun and interesting to attend your program.

3. Help keep track of personal items (such as boots, hats, mittens, and blankets) so families don't need to replace them.

4. Provide a nurturing relationship outside of the family.

5. Share positive or humorous stories about the child with the parent to bridge the gap between your program and home.

6. Believe that all parents want what is best for their children.

7. Accept differences in child rearing, family traditions, and parenting styles.

8. Remember that parents are doing the best they can. It is always easier to criticize than to walk in someone else's shoes.

9. Communicate early about concerns, before resentment builds.

10. Use problem-solving strategies to approach difficult situations.

11. Keep information confidential.

12. Talk positively about family members in front of the child.

Foreword

As a parent and former provider, nothing causes me more self-doubts about my skills and abilities than when I confront challenging behavior in young children. Some of my experiences with young children trigger in my head the words to the familiar nursery rhyme: "I once knew a little girl with a curl in the middle of her forehead, when she was good, she was very, very good; and when she was bad she was horrid." The "she" can become a "he" for me very easily! No gender bias here.

What Deborah Hewitt manages to do for me in her book *So This Is Normal Too* is take away the value judgment of good and horrid. The book gives me the skills to focus on teaching young children the behavior skills they need to make their life—and my life—better. Deborah Hewitt's techniques build confidence in both of us.

Where do these difficult behaviors come from? A child may be hungry, ill, or tired. He or she may be dealing with developmental changes of just growing up. We all struggle with this. External elements as well may be affecting the child. A parent may be out of town, Grandma may be ill, a new child in the child care setting may have taken away a best friend, or the phases of the moon may be changing. The list is endless. *So This Is Normal Too* helps to identify the factors we can control in the environment that may have an immediate positive response from the child. Some factors may not change and *So This Is Normal Too* gives us useful techniques to help the young child confidently cope and continue life's journey in a sometimes difficult world.

The real strength of this book is facilitating communication between parents and providers through creative problem solving. The parent and provider build a trusting relationship by focusing on a specific behavior of the child and jointly coming up with an action plan based on the best interest of the child. Often, tension between the parent and the provider is not on the outcome or goal they have for the child, but on the method for obtaining the goal. *So This Is Normal Too* gives both the parent and provider the same base of information. From there, they can work together to design an action plan and achieve the goal. The Plan for Action is a tool that focuses on behavior, building confidence and esteem for the parent, the provider, and, most importantly, the child.

Deborah Hewitt has successfully created a valuable resource that will be used again and again.

BARBARA O'SULLIVAN, M.A.
Former teacher, early childhood
specialist, trainer and director,
past president,
Minnesota AEYC

Preface

Hearing the frustrations voiced by parents and people working with young children convinced me of the need for this book. As a parent and provider, I know how disturbing difficult behaviors can be. I find it particularly upsetting when I think I have one troublesome behavior under control only to discover that another one has taken its place. For me, guiding behavior becomes a constant challenge that requires me to improve my problem-solving abilities and my guidance skills.

When a problem behavior arises with our own children or children we work with, we tend to lose our objectivity. Our emotions cloud our vision and make it harder to determine what to do. This book is written to help parents and people working with preschool-aged children focus on solutions to common behavioral situations.

When parents and providers share the responsibility of caring for a child, they must work together. Resources for Child Caring recognized the need for a resource that would give providers and parents developmental information and assist them in responding to a child's behavior. A grant funded by the Northwest Area Foundation in 1986 gave birth to the original book, *So This Is Normal*. That book's goals were to provide practical information that reflected sound child development concepts.

In *So This Is Normal Too*, the goal remains the same: to provide information about behaviors that are common to preschool-aged children. Another goal is to promote understanding and consistency between providers and parents. This book goes beyond the original by offering many more topics and suggestions.

When you face a behavioral challenge, *So This Is Normal Too* encourages you to step back and look at the situation objectively. Each chapter offers a number of viable suggestions for dealing with the challenges you experience. Finally, this book provides a framework as you work with others to determine the most effective guidance strategies for your situation.

Included in this book are sixteen challenging behaviors those attending guiding behavior classes most frequently describe to me. Each chapter is divided into three parts. First, you'll find information for the provider. At the urging of many providers, similar information for the parent follows. These sections contain basically the same information but are written with language and examples specific to each reader. Equipped with this common base of information, parents and providers are ready for the third section, "A Plan for Action." Using the plan for action and problem-solving techniques, parents and providers can work together to decide how to help a child learn appropriate behaviors.

Although you'll read about the frustrations of providers and parents in each chapter, this book focuses on solving problems. The ideas offered reflect a guidance approach to behavior management. The solutions are expressions of the underlying theory. As you consistently and conscientiously apply the techniques, the theory becomes second nature. A brief description of guidance theory is presented in the introduction. If you do not understand the foundations of a guidance approach or are unsure why a recommendation is made, I encourage you to do further study.

A number of early childhood settings and many parents have used the suggestions included in this book successfully. The ideas are not all inclusive but will help you start thinking about your own solutions. Be sure to add your ideas. Your efforts may not be realized on the first day, in the first week, or even in the first month; but when you offer support and guidance, you show a child that you believe in him and that he is worth the effort.

This book is intended for parents and people providing services to young children in a variety of settings, including child care centers, family child care homes, preschools, Early Childhood Family Education programs, special education programs, Head Start programs, parent cooperatives, play groups, and religious education programs. No one term best fits all those providing services to young children in such a wide variety of settings. Therefore "early childhood settings," "providers," and "parents" have been chosen to refer to those who might find this book helpful.

Most of the behaviors and the suggestions for dealing with them are common to the preschool-aged child (two-and-a-half to six years old). However, the behaviors and suggestions are broad enough to be helpful for slightly older or younger age groups as well. Those new to the field of early childhood education or to parenting will find the suggestions insightful as well as filled with common sense. People who have worked or lived with children for a number of years will find the suggestions worth revisiting when a situation momentarily baffles them.

Because both boys and girls display the behaviors described, "he" and "she" are used in alternating chapters.

Permission is given to each purchaser to reproduce copies as needed to hand out to a parent within your own program (or to your provider). Programs with more than one site should purchase a book for each location. Permission to reprint for any other use must be obtained from Redleaf Press.

Many people have helped to make this book possible. First and most importantly thanks goes to my husband, Jeff, who has always believed in me. I greatly appreciate his never ending support, encouragement, and willingness to take on additional responsibilities to allow me the time to work on this project. My children, Marcie and Reid, contributed to the book by providing me with lots of practical experiences and behavior challenges to ponder. They also bring me great joy and necessary breaks from the consuming work of writing a book.

The providers taking my guiding behavior classes always teach me something. The children in my preschool classes provide me with humbling experiences as well as reminders that each individual must be treated in his or her own unique fashion. Linda Farnum provided exceptional care to my son so I might concentrate on my writing.

I am grateful to all the readers who have given me valuable feedback and helped to make this a better book: Shelley Beardsley, Judy Davis, Stacey Dunn, Sherry Haaf, Sandy Heidemann, Cindy Kelly, Leigh Ostrander, Barbara O'Sullivan, Carolyn Ronneberg, Ann Ruff, and Caroline Winget.

Finally, appreciation goes to my editor, Eileen Nelson, for valuing my thoughts, providing advice, and offering encouragement throughout the project.

Introduction

Getting children to behave is the most difficult part of my job.

—Teacher in a classroom of four year olds

I never knew parenting would be so hard.

—Father of a three year old

What is the greatest challenge in working or living with young children? Ask that question of parents or providers and many will tell you that guiding behavior is the greatest one. As young children learn about the world around them and the complexities of relationships, they make behavioral mistakes. It can be difficult to know how to put an end to some of these and teach children more acceptable behaviors. *So This Is Normal Too* offers guidelines that make it easier to care for children who are displaying normal yet challenging behaviors.

As a provider or parent, you have an opportunity to teach a child about caring relationships. When you create a nurturing relationship and provide a variety of experiences, a child discovers the joy of learning, masters skills needed to interact with others, finds appropriate ways to get his needs met, and learns to effectively communicate. You have an awesome responsibility! The way you guide a child's behavior affects his ability and willingness to learn these important skills. Guiding behavior is a crucial part of any adult-child relationship. You can meet the challenges of guiding behavior by observing the child, applying basic behavior guidance techniques, and using problem-solving strategies.

A Guidance Approach

Children need to be guided and taught about behavior in a way that protects self-esteem. Think about the child who always seems out of sync with the group or family. How many messages does this child get about behavior? Are the messages mostly positive or negative? Do they build a positive self-image or break it down?

José is a child who has difficulty participating in large group activities at child care. He isn't particularly interested in stories, blurts out responses that aren't related to the topic at hand, and wiggles and fidgets throughout group time. Bobbie, his child care provider, calls his name often, reminds him to pay attention, and scolds him when he isn't doing what is expected of the group. José receives a number of messages about his behavior and his skills that are not very positive. These messages could leave him thinking group learning experiences aren't fun. What if he decides he's no good at it and stops trying? A real possibility.

Bobbie can do many things to help José avoid this type of thinking and learn more adaptive behaviors. She can make sure José knows what is expected of him at group time. (This may be his first experience with group activities or the first time someone has taken time to explain it to him.) Bobbie could do more finger plays, flannelboard stories, or puppet shows to make group time more stimulating and interactive. She can arrange for story time to follow outside play or a movement activity so he is ready to sit for a short time. Bobbie can make sure she comments on his behavior or gives him the thumbs up signal when he is doing a good job.

José's parents are frustrated with his activity level at home too. José sits for only short periods of time. He looks at a toy for a couple of minutes, then drops it in pursuit of something new. He doesn't read books for long. During meals, he moves about and wiggles so much that he often spills. Again José is in trouble if traditional responses to behavior are used.

José's parents can help him by making sure he has plenty of time outside to be physically active. They might find ways to let José be active indoors by setting up activities such as throwing newspaper balls into a box, playing baseball with a foam bat and ball, or playing catch with an inflatable ball. To lengthen his attention span with toys, José's parents can make sure he is challenged by his toys. They can also play with

> Your role in a guidance approach is complex. You must:
>
> 1. Develop a supportive relationship.
> 2. Project a confident attitude that assumes the child will learn appropriate behavior.
> 3. Observe the behavior, then consider factors that may be contributing to a problem.
> 4. Plan the environment.
> 5. Arrange the schedule.
> 6. Plan the difficulty of activities.
> 7. Teach acceptable behavior.
> 8. Work with others to arrive at solutions to problems.

José and expand upon his play ideas. To encourage interest in reading, his parents might choose nursery rhymes and stories with repetitive phrases so he can say them along with the reader. Or they could look for fast-paced stories that appeal to his interest in action. Spills are to be expected as young children learn to feed themselves. However, some may be prevented by making sure José's chair is the right size for him (maybe a booster is needed) and offering a half glass of the beverage. A supply of paper towels can be kept handy so he can help clean up any mess.

When you support a child in the ways described above, you are taking a guidance approach to teaching behavior. This approach focuses on building nurturing relationships, preventing inappropriate behavior, finding ways to solve problems, and working with others to help the child.

Develop a Supportive Relationship

Your relationship with a child is essential. When children feel safe, valued, and accepted, they are more likely to behave in acceptable ways. Build a strong relationship with all children. Rebuild or strengthen your relationship with a child who is experiencing behavioral difficulties.

To build or strengthen your relationship with a child, spend one-on-one time. Learn his likes and dislikes. Plan his favorite meal or activities. Take an interest in him and his activities. Play next to him. Follow his play suggestions. Enjoy things you have in common. Share an innocent secret or something funny. In addition, providers can have things with which he is familiar available to him.

Project a Confident Attitude

Your attitude when you deal with behavioral difficulties deserves careful consideration. How you think and feel about a behavior and toward a child is the foundation of a guidance approach. You will respond quite differently if you think a child is out to get you or purposefully misbehaving than if you believe he is confused, unaware, or inexperienced. For example, if a child is playing in a plastic tub filled with cornmeal and spills some, you could assume she is being sloppy and doesn't care about keeping things clean. Or you could assume she is having so much fun she doesn't realize the cornmeal is flying.

Depending upon your attitude, you are likely to choose very different ways to handle this situation. Your tone of voice, facial expressions, and body language will reflect your feelings. These subtleties may speak louder than the words you use. If you believe the child is being oppositional, you are more likely to go to her with a stern face and use a demanding voice to tell her, "You need to clean up this mess. Come on, get busy. *Come! Now!*" Statements like these, and the manner in which they are said, suggest you are fed up and perhaps do not have enough strategies to use in coping with this situation.

On the other hand, if you believe this child needs to learn to clean up things that she messes, but you do not view it as naughty or misbehavior, you would use a matter-of-fact manner and encourage her as you speak. You might say, "When you were playing, some of the cornmeal fell out. I need you to clean up your spills. Here is the whisk broom and the dustpan. I'll use the broom and help." In the second scenario, you are assuming the child was not aware of the mess and that she needed more information or a direction to clean up. By responding in this way, you have taught her that she is responsible and that she can do many things for herself.

Observe the Behavior

Providers and parents have so many demands for their attention that they usually have time for only hurried glimpses of children. You can miss vital information about a behavior problem and draw incorrect conclusions, however. Take a step back and assess the situation.

Watch this child carefully. Look for his strengths (you may find there are many areas in which the child is doing just fine). Consider the areas in which the child needs to improve. Watch other children too. Providers can look at other children in their program who are approximately the same age and temperament. Parents can arrange a time to observe their child and others in the early childhood setting or informally observe children in their neighborhood. Other children are likely to behave in similar ways. Perhaps their disputes are not as obvious or perhaps they just avoid getting caught. Take a look. This child's behavior may not be what you first thought.

Ask yourself the following general questions as you watch a child having difficulty (specific questions are included in each chapter): Under what circumstances is the behavior taking place? Who else is involved? Does it take place at certain times of the day or during certain activities? What happens right before the behavior? What takes place immediately following? Does this child have the skills needed for the task? How much verbal or nonverbal communication is taking place?

When you observe, take notes for your own records as well as to share with others. Use descriptive words and phrases. Try to recreate the situation on paper. Use objective terms that do not place judgments on what is taking place. For example, in observing Tyler, record, "Tyler stands at the sandbox. He does not respond to Sue's comments. He looks down. He draws circles with his car." These are facts that are observable to all. Be careful not to include judgments in your description of what is taking place. If you write, "Tyler pouts. He stands at the sandbox and ignores Sue when she talks to him," you are judging what is taking place.

In addition to your written narratives of behaviors, you may want to count the number of times a behavior occurs during a given time period. How many times does this child bite in one week? one day? one hour? At the same time you log situations you are concerned about, be sure to record examples of times a child handles a difficult situation well. Recording a child's strengths as well as when he needs help provides balance and helps you to keep your perspective.

Observe three to four times before making judgments or drawing any conclusions. If you observe only once, your conclusions may not be accurate. The child's behavior may be influenced by an oncoming cold, a fight with a sibling, or a grandparent's visit. These and many other factors can cause the child to behave in a way that is not typical or does not show him at his best. Even after careful observation, you may not know the cause of a behavior. It isn't always possible or necessary to determine a cause. You can still make plans that are sensitive to a child's needs and help him learn appropriate behaviors.

Your observations become the basis of your plans to help a child. You will tailor your response to the individual by using what you have learned about him. Analyze the information you have gathered to find ways to avoid problems; identify what the child needs to learn; and gain insight about how to teach it.

Plan the Environment

Arranging the environment is an important element in teaching a child independence and self-control. Children need a pleasant space in which they can move about safely. They need an envi-

---

The information you gain from your observations will help you:

- Identify skill strengths and areas that need improvement.
- Find insights into behaviors.
- Determine how to proceed.
- Talk with others about the behavior.
- Gauge if you are making progress.
- Gain perspective.

Many factors can affect a child's behavior. Sometimes, you're fortunate enough to be aware of the influences. Many times you don't find out what is taking place until after a difficult time. Other times you never find out. Some factors can be controlled while others cannot. Some possible influences that can affect a child's behavior are listed below.

- Changes in routine, providers, or at home
- Frustration
- Boredom
- Feeling too crowded
- Lack of language skills
- Fatigue
- Overstimulation

- Hunger
- Illness or oncoming illness
- Illness of a family member
- Need for attention
- Adult expectations that are too high
- Adult expectations that are too low

- Taking a medication
- An allergy
- Poor social skills
- Disagreement with a friend, sibling, or adult
- Visit from a relative
- Anticipation of an upcoming activity

ronment that allows them to explore and actively engage in developmentally appropriate activities. Their environment should be organized in a way that allows them to make choices and do many things for themselves.

A change in the environment can be a simple and effective way to take care of some problems. When a behavior problem arises, consider how you might change your environment to avoid the situation or cut back on the number of times it occurs. For example, parents may be able to place hooks at the child's level so he can hang his jacket up instead of leaving it on the floor. In the early childhood setting, a provider might use a seating arrangement or put more space between children who are having difficulty sitting next to one another at group time.

Consider ways to avoid behavior problems by critically examining your space. A few of the questions you might ask yourself include: Are materials and toys available to the child so he can make independent play choices? Are there too many things, making it difficult for the child to choose? Are there enough things to occupy this child? Is the play space large enough for the activity?

Arrange the Schedule
Much of the success of your day is dependent on the schedule and routines you establish. Consistent routines let children know what to expect and can feel comforting. Create a schedule that

alternates strenuous and restful activities to help children pace themselves throughout the day. Balance child-choice activities with adult-directed activities to help children learn both independence and interactive skills. Make it clear where children are to go and what they are to do during changes in activity (that is, you might say, "Put your coat on and wait for me by the door"). Reduce confusion by keeping things similar from day to day. Your schedule, however, must not be so rigid that it cannot be changed if a problem occurs. Change the schedule by a few minutes so a hungry child can eat, a tired child can rest, and a frustrated child can take a break.

Plan Developmentally Appropriate Activities
Children learn best when they are actively involved with materials. If an activity offered is too hard, a child may act out because he is feeling frustrated or inadequate. Materials that are too easy may be uninteresting and lead to wandering or inactivity. Take care to have toys and activities available that match a child's developmental level. When behavior problems appear, consider how you might change the activity to better meet the needs of the child. How can you adapt it so it matches the child's skill level? How can you make it participatory to capture the child's attention? How will you shorten it for a child who is unable to sit for very long?

Teach Acceptable Behavior

In a guidance approach to behavior, it is your responsibility to decide what skills the child needs in order to more effectively handle a situation the next time it occurs. If you try to eliminate an undesirable behavior, you cannot assume the child will know what to do instead. The child needs your help to learn the appropriate behavior.

Decide what to teach by watching what this child is currently doing in difficult situations. You probably know what you don't want him to do. Now identify what you want him to do instead. For instance, if a child is hitting when he doesn't get a turn with a toy, teach him to come and get you for help with turn taking or use words to get a turn. Set a goal. Be as specific as possible. Focus on a new behavior or increasing a behavior you see occasionally. Example goals are listed in the Plan for Action found at the end of each chapter.

Once you have decided what to teach, you must decide how you will teach it. Each chapter of this book gives you many strategies. As you read, you will think of your own ideas. Parents and providers will want to work together to develop a Plan for Action. As you develop your plan, consider how you will avoid the problem, what words you will use when working with the child, what activities you will do to help the child practice new skills, and how you will respond to mistaken behavior.

Working with Others

It is critical that parents and providers work together to solve behavioral difficulties. Build a positive relationship from the very beginning. Share information about the child in each setting. One family child care provider made a mental note of something entertaining or interesting that the child did each day to share with parents. This helped the parents know the provider was tuned in to their child as well as helped to bridge the gap between child care and home.

Some parents want to know about the eating, sleeping, and toileting habits of their child. Some are more interested in the social relationships the child is building. Others want to know about the activities in which their child was involved. Providers can find out what types of information the parent is most interested in and keep them up-to-date. Parents can support their provider by sharing information that may be helpful in caring for a child (for example, changing sleep patterns or stressful situations in the child's life). When you need to share information, be sure you do so confidentially. Explain to the child, "I need to talk with your provider (parent) alone." Then walk out of hearing distance. Or set a time to talk either in person or on the phone without the child nearby.

Many times parents and providers rely on notes or try to talk about problems at drop-off or pickup. Things are generally hectic during this time; parents are in a hurry, children are tired, and providers may be frustrated after dealing with the behavior. It is better to arrange a time to meet to discuss a difficult behavior. Say, "I have noticed that Nathan is swearing a lot lately. I would like to talk with you about it. When can you meet in the next two or three days?" It is best if the meeting is not during a time when the child needs attention (options may be naptime or during a provider's preparation time). Set aside enough time to talk without interruption.

Many times providers dread having to talk with parents about a problem. Parents have similar feelings about discussing a problem with their provider. Both parties have a right to honest communication that fosters a partnership in caring for a child. Don't wait until you are frustrated with a behavior to begin to talk about it. People need time to digest information and think about how they will respond. Usually it is best to talk when you first see a behavior pattern developing.

Keep your expectations about what can be done in each setting realistic. Most parents can see to it that their child is well fed and well rested. They may be able to do little about biting if the problem seems related to the group experience and is taking place only in the early childhood setting. It is ineffective for parents to punish a child for something that has taken place hours earlier. Expectations about what providers can do must be realistic too. Most providers will do all they can to respond to the individual needs of a child. However, they are unlikely to implement complicated or time-consuming requests; not because they are unwilling to help, but because of the numerous demands on their time and attention.

Providers need to recognize the emotional investment parents have in their children. Parents need to realize providers are sensitive about the work they do with children. The information you share may feel like a personal attack if you are not careful to phrase things sensitively. Use good judgment as you decide how many of your concerns to share in your first discussion. It is better to talk about digestible pieces of information than to alienate the other from further discussion.

Keep a positive attitude toward working together. Build a cooperative effort by viewing challenging behaviors as something you can work out together. Be careful to avoid blaming the behavior on anyone. This is unproductive, builds resentment, and leads to defensiveness. Attend to the situation at hand and determine what can be done to improve it.

How to Use This Book

So This Is Normal Too discusses behaviors that cause concern to parents and providers alike. Certainly behaviors such as biting, hitting, and temper tantrums are upsetting. Most often these and the other behaviors described in this book are considered "normal." Knowing that a behavior is normal doesn't always make it easier to deal with, however. Providers and parents must accept mistaken behaviors while helping children learn behaviors that allow them to be successful in social situations.

Each chapter in *So This Is Normal Too* is divided into three sections. The first section, "For Providers," contains information about how the behavior may look in an early childhood setting and provides suggestions for the provider to use. The second section, "For Parent(s)," offers similar information for parents. This section is written with the family situation in mind and has examples of how the behavior may present itself at home. You will find that these sections are purposefully alike and provide the parent and provider with a similar base of information. You may reproduce copies as needed to hand to a parent within your program (or your provider).

Each of these first two sections contains five smaller sections.

What Is It? This section provides a description of the behavior. When possible, you'll find an age at which the behavior typically presents itself. This will help you judge if the behavior of the child is characteristic or out of place.

Observe and Problem Solve. You are encouraged to observe the child to gather information about what is taking place and helpful actions to take. You'll find observation questions to pose and suggestions based on developmentally appropriate practices. The practices help to avoid problem situations and respond to those situations that cannot be avoided.

Work with the Parent(s)/Work with Your Provider. Suggestions on working together are included in both the provider and the parent sections. In the section for the providers, you'll find information to help support parents and understand their point of view. In the parent section, you'll find information about the realities of caring for a group of children and how this differs from a family situation. Knowing these facts begins honest communication regarding the guidance techniques that can be used in each setting.

When to Get Help. You'll read about the guidelines to follow regarding when to seek professional help, including indicators that a child may need help. You'll also find general suggestions regarding whom to contact.

For Further Reading. When behaviors are challenging, try to gather as much information as possible. Each chapter lists suggested readings that provide more information on the topic or related topics.

The book's third section, "A Plan for Action," completes each chapter and helps providers and parents develop a course of action. Use the Plan for Action as a summary, a basis for discussion, or a formal agreement signed by both parties. The plans contain two parts: an overview of the suggestions contained in the chapter and a reproducible planning form.

The overview contains goals to work toward and ideas for both providers and parents. Most ideas are found here (in a few chapters, all ideas are listed in this category). This list helps providers and parents focus on the things they can do to promote consistency between the early childhood setting and home. When parents and providers use the same strategies, the child receives clear messages about behavior and is less confused. Following these ideas are a few suggestions specific to the group situation. Finally, actions to be taken by the parent are listed.

The following provides you with a sequence of steps to take as you use this book and work to resolve behavioral challenges.

Read Appropriate Chapters

Behaviors are complex and a problem can be multifaceted. As you face a difficult situation, you may find that more than one chapter applies. Read all those that are related to the problem you are experiencing. Piece the appropriate information together and reflect on what is taking place.

Each chapter poses a number of questions to guide you as you observe and prepare to meet the individual's needs. Read the information presented under each observation question (even if you don't think the question applies one hundred percent). Many of the suggestions listed under one question will be useful in a number of situations.

Observe the Child

Devote time to systematically observe the child who is having difficulty. Use the recommendations for observing presented earlier. In addition, ask yourself the specific questions in each chapter as you gather more information about what is taking place.

Apply General Guidance Strategies

Next, apply general guidance strategies. Build or rebuild your relationship. Adjust your attitude. Change aspects of your environment, schedule, or activities to avoid problems. If the difficulties persist, continue with the following procedure.

Give the Parent (or Provider) the Material Written for Them

Before the parent (or provider) will be able to discuss a behavior with you, they will need time to think about it. If you have already been concerned by a behavior, you may have moved ahead in your thinking. It may take some time for the other person to recognize examples of the behavior in their setting and to decide how they would like to approach the situation. Give the other person the reading material written for them. Allow a week or two to study the information.

Meet to Develop a Plan for Action

Arrange a meeting with the parent (or provider). When you meet, set an expectant tone that you will be able to solve the situation when you work together. A sample agenda follows.

- Describe the child's behavior; provide specific examples.
- Set a goal for the child.
- Brainstorm a list of possible solutions.
- Decide those you will try first.
- Agree to put the plan into action.
- Set a date to check in and discuss progress.

When a child engages in a challenging behavior:

1. Read all the materials on a behavior as well as other behaviors that are closely related.

2. Observe and gather more detailed information.

3. Apply general guidance strategies. Attend to your relationship and attitude. Avoid problems by changing aspects of your environment, schedule, and activities.

If difficulties persist and this behavior is demonstrated routinely:

4. Give the parent/provider the material written for them.

5. Arrange a meeting so you can work together. Develop a Plan for Action.

6. Put your plan into action.

7. Observe again.

8. Meet to discuss progress.

9. Modify your plan if necessary.

10. Go to step 6.

Describe the Behavior. Begin your meeting by describing the behaviors you see in your setting. Provide specific, factual examples from your observations. Include behaviors that are appropriate as well as those that concern you. Ask if the other person sees similar behaviors; chances are they do. Sometimes, however, children behave very differently in different settings. Even if the other person doesn't see the behaviors you are concerned about, most will do all they can to help the child learn appropriate behavior.

Set a Goal. Develop one or two goals for the child by using the information you have learned about him, what you know of your environment, program goals, your values, and those values held by your community. Focus on what the child needs to learn. When a child engages in more of an appropriate behavior, a decrease in inappropriate behavior is likely to take place. Concentrating on what the child needs to learn helps you take a guidance approach and frames the goal in positive language.

You'll find sample goals in the "Plan for Action" part of each chapter. You can also write other goals that more closely reflect the needs of the individual with whom you are working. If the child is demonstrating more than one difficult behavior, you may need to prioritize and decide which to address first. How well a child needs to perform a goal is not described in the examples. This must be decided on an individual basis. Keep your expectations realistic. Look for improvement in behavior not perfection.

Brainstorm Solutions. After setting a goal, providers and parents will want to brainstorm a number of solutions. List as many ideas as you can that will teach the goal behavior. Begin with the suggestions given in each chapter and summarized in the "Plan for Action" section. These suggestions are based on sound child development theory and generally are effective in reducing difficulties. They offer ways to reduce mistaken behaviors and teach a child to control his own behavior. Add your own ideas.

In a few of the chapters, a suggestion is listed in more than one place on the Plan for Action. For example, in chapter 1 the suggestion "Be responsible for behavior" is listed under ac-

tions for the provider and under actions for the parents to take. Providers and parents must decide which is best for their situation.

Decide on a Plan. The focus of your meeting should be to decide on a plan. Determine which of the ideas are most appropriate to your situation. Write three or four actions you will both take on the reproducible planning form provided in the Plan for Action. Write additional techniques to be used at home or in the early childhood setting. Be careful not to overwhelm yourself or the child with too many changes at once. The techniques can be difficult to implement as well as difficult to know which of the changes were most helpful and are most important to continue.

Complete the planning form by setting a date six weeks to three months (depending on the urgency of the situation) from the time of your discussion to meet again. Signatures on the Plan for Action are optional unless you are using the form as an agreement. Information on using the Plan for Action as an agreement follows in the discussion of "When Parents and Providers Can't Come to Agreement" later in this introduction.

Be respectful of the other party's time commitments and end the meeting on time. Be sure to communicate positive expectations that together you will be able to teach the child more adaptive skills.

Put Your Plan into Action

After your meeting, apply the strategies to which you agreed. Use your copy of the Plan for Action as a reminder to do the activities or use the words you have prepared. Post your plan in a place where you are sure to see it. (Of course, in a setting where people are coming and going, keep the reminder confidential. Perhaps you can put it inside a cupboard door that you open often.)

Once you have developed your Plan for Action, limit daily conversation about behavior. If you need to vent frustration, find someone outside of the situation who can provide a listening ear. A coworker, family member, director, or mentor may be able to provide support.

Observe Again

Observe the child again a week or two before your next meeting so you have current, accurate information to share. Look for progress and behaviors that need continued improvement.

Meet to Discuss Progress

The purpose of your second meeting (and perhaps additional ones too), is to decide if the child's behavior has improved and if your strategies are helpful. When you evaluate, you may find that the child has made good progress toward the goal you set. If so, pat yourselves on the back and congratulate each other for helping the child over this hurdle. Other times, you may find the child has made progress but continued work is needed.

Modify Your Plan

If you have continued work to do, reevaluate your goal. Make sure the goal is appropriate for this child; also evaluate if you are expecting too much. Adapt or change your strategies. Eliminate those that are ineffective and replace them with ones you think will be more helpful. Agree once again to check with each other in two to three months. You may need to repeat the planning and implementing cycle a few times before you see progress. Behavior change is neither quick nor easy. It takes time and patience. You can still expect mistakes to occur even after considerable growth.

You may recognize many of the steps described above as those used in problem solving. By using these steps, you will find that there are a number of possible solutions to one situation. The trick is to find the one solution—or solutions—that best match your situation.

Reasons Plans Are Ineffective. Some of the suggestions for dealing with a difficult behavior call for changes in routine, activity, environment, or your responses. Keep an open mind as you consider which of the suggestions will help this child and which you can implement. Change is often met with resistance. Yet when you make the effort and see how successful you can be in preventing problems, you will find it well worth the effort. For some children, the change may mean the difference between success and continued frustration. Among the rea-

---

Both adults and children can find the steps in problem solving helpful as they approach a difficult situation. Use the following steps as you work to resolve a behavioral issue. Teach children to use the steps when in a conflict.

Steps in Problem Solving

1. Identify the problem.
2. Gather information.
3. Generate solutions.
4. Choose the best one or ones. Decide on a plan.
5. Implement your plan.
6. Evaluate how your plan is working.
7. Revise your plan as needed.

Helpful Phrases

1. "I see_____" (Describe what you see taking place. For example, "I see you both want a turn on the swing.")
2. "Tell me about your argument."
3. "What could you do to work this out?" or "How could you work this out so you're both happy?"
4. "What might happen if you tried that idea?" or "Which idea will you try first?"
5. "Try it."
6. "Is that idea working?"
7. "Is there another idea that might work?" or "Is there an idea that will work better?"

sons plans for changing behavior are ineffective are an unwillingness on the part of the adult to try a different approach and discontinuing the use of a plan too soon.

When to Get Help

Some children do not learn to control inappropriate behaviors as quickly as others. Their behaviors don't significantly decrease even though the techniques suggested are usually successful. The behaviors may be more severe, more frequent, or persist for a longer period of time. These children may need additional help. You will find guidelines about when to seek assistance in both the provider and parent sections of each chapter. General information follows.

Parents know their children well and are often the first to notice a problem. Providers are in a unique position and can recognize problems too. Sometimes they notice a problem because it is a behavior demonstrated only in a group of peers. Other times a behavior or skill lag becomes apparent in the early childhood setting because of the academic type of activities offered. With early recognition and intervention, many children can get the help they need to be better prepared for a formal school setting.

When you are concerned about a child's pattern of behavior, follow the steps described in each chapter, including developing a Plan for Action. Allow enough time to see a decrease in mistaken behavior and time for the child to learn a new behavior. In many cases, you will need to give your efforts four to six months before you see improvement.

Many of the Plans for Action suggest that you get help by learning more about a behavior. Attend classes or workshops. Read the suggested materials included in each chapter. Look for books and journals in your public library, college or university library, or the library of a nearby Early Childhood and Family Education program. Talk with a colleague, mentor, or family member. Providers can ask a consultant or parent educator to help develop strategies specific to their situation. Be sure to obtain written permission from a parent before doing this. Share any information with the parent that would benefit the child at home.

If the behavior remains a problem, despite your efforts, you may want to have this child see a specialist. Deciding to make a referral can be a difficult decision for providers. Deciding to seek this level of help is also difficult for parents. Additional help does not indicate that you were unsuccessful. Instead seeking additional help means you recognized the limits of your setting or of your own expertise.

The referral process can be very complicated. Specialists to contact include the family's primary health care provider, the school district, county or state mental health department, or private agencies. General suggestions are made in each chapter. Start with these and ask what other services might be available in your community. Gather the names and phone numbers of support services. Make calls to obtain more information before deciding on options. After meeting with a specialist, parents should discuss with their provider any information learned that would be helpful to them as they care for the child.

Economic factors prevent some people from obtaining needed services. If this is a barrier, look for programs that base their fees on family income. Service organizations such as the Shriners, Kiwanis, and the Salvation Army are examples of groups that may be able to provide financial help. There may be additional ones in your community.

A provider's observation records of the child's behavior can be helpful to specialists. This information, when it has been written objectively, can be a critical piece of data collected. Providers might offer to send their notes or talk directly to the specialist about the concerns they have. Written permission from the parent must be obtained before releasing any information. Parents can request that their provider prepare this type of information so they can present it as part of the background data too.

When Providers and Parents Can't Come to Agreement

Sometimes parents and providers don't agree about a problem. Many reasons exist for this disagreement. The parent may not see the behavior at home. The behavior may not be a problem when there are only one or two children to care for as in some families. Parents may not understand the dynamics of caring for a group of children. Parents may deny the existence of a problem they are unprepared to confront.

Providers may view a normal behavior as a problem because of the demands of caring for a group of children. Sometimes a behavior that is acceptable at home is difficult to allow in the group setting because of the increased noise level, activity level, or number of disputes it seems to cause. Providers may have difficulties because they ask too much of a child. They may be uncomfortable around this child. Perhaps they are inflexible in scheduling or unaccepting of individual differences. Value or cultural differences may also be a part of any disagreement.

Obviously, when there is a disagreement, providers and parents will want to reach some sort of compromise that benefits the child. At the heart of any conversation should be "What is best for the child?" Focusing on the child will help both parties reduce defensiveness.

Providers and parents may have differing opinions on how to approach a situation. Be flexible in your planning. Respect the other person's thoughts and ideas. Perhaps you can agree to try something until your next meeting. Take note if it is helpful and continue it or explain

why it didn't work and decide on something more effective. Don't agree to ideas that are unkind, unethical, or impractical. Reject the idea firmly but kindly saying, "I don't think that would benefit him the most" or "I'm not able to do that." Providers must keep their state regulations in mind as they determine a Plan for Action. Your state may require you to do something different from what is recommended in this book or what a parent recommends. Your licensing takes priority over these suggestions.

If the parent or the provider you are working with chooses not to work with you at this point, this book can still serve as a valuable tool. Read it yourself. Apply the strategies presented and continue to work toward better behavior. If in a few months you still see behaviors that concern you, bring them up again.

Sometimes a Plan for Action may call for the parent to contact a specialist or for the provider to contact a consultant. In situations in which there is a great deal of disagreement or when there has been little cooperation between parties, you may need to use the Plan for Action as an agreement to ensure these important recommendations are carried out. In these concerning cases, the continuation of your relationship may become contingent upon obtaining these services before your next meeting.

On rare occasions, it may become necessary for parents and providers to assess if the child's enrollment in a program continues to be in his best interest. Providers need to consider if they are continuing to treat this child with respect and if they are offering him high quality services. Parents need to evaluate if the child is receiving the best possible care in this setting. Terminating services is not a solution to all problems, but in some cases may be best for the child.

If a provider asks a family to find a new program, it may relieve one set of frustrations but may not be a cure all. Providers need to develop skills that will enable them to effectively deal with all types of behaviors. The child who joins the program next may bring new behavioral challenges.

Parents may be tempted to change programs rather than face problems being brought to their attention. Sometimes a change can alleviate problems. More often, when the child doesn't learn more effective behaviors, the problems follow. In fact, the feelings resulting from a change may complicate matters and make it more difficult for a child to cope.

Parents and providers need to examine their motives for considering the termination of services. Legitimate reasons are those that focus on the best interest of the child.

Conclusion

Guiding the behavior of young children can be very challenging. You will find it easier if you look for ways to avoid difficulties and teach children appropriate behaviors. When you take the time to observe, analyze, and determine a Plan for Action, you can do much to help a child learn effective behaviors that will last a lifetime. Your support and guidance helps a child fit into social situations and starts him on the road to future success.

CHAPTER 1

Don't Go Mommy: Separating

Anna has been coming here for weeks. Now all of a sudden she cries every time her mom drops her off. I don't understand what is going on.

What Is It?

One of a child's first experiences separating from her parent comes when someone else cares for her. Fear of being separated can be stressful for the child whether the separation is for a short or long period. A child periodically experiences developmental peaks in separation anxiety. A number of these peaks take place during the infant and toddler years. This chapter focuses on preschool-aged children. For information on how to help infants and toddlers develop healthy attachments to others and cope with separation, read *Character Development: Encouraging Self-Esteem & Self-Discipline in Infants, Toddlers, and Two-Year-Olds* by Polly Greenberg (NAEYC, 1991), and other similar references.

Most likely, all preschool-aged children experience some feelings of separation anxiety. The degree to which they show their feelings varies depending upon their personality and previous experiences with separation. Some children approach a new setting enthusiastically, seemingly unaffected by the separation. Others become upset, cry, or cling to the parent when it is time for them to leave. A few children withdraw and refuse to engage in activities or talk. Helping an anxious child cope and deal with her feelings is an important step in guiding her toward independence.

Observe and Problem Solve

Ask the following questions as you watch a child's response to your setting. The suggestions will help you formulate a plan to ease a child's concerns and help her build healthy attachments to new providers.

➤ *Does this child become upset, cry, or fuss when she is left with new providers?*

This is a normal reaction to being left the first few times. Ease this child into your program before beginning the normal schedule. Offer an orientation and phase-in period where the parent and child visit the program. (If a parent isn't available, perhaps a grandparent or other trusted adult could substitute.) The first visit can be quite short. On following days, the child and parent can attend together and gradually lengthen their stay. The parent should play near the child at first, then move to the side of the room to serve as a safe base from which to operate. Once the child seems comfortable, the parent can say good-bye and take a short walk or read a book in the car. The length of time spent away from the child can be increased each time until the child is able to stay for the whole program day. The length of the phase-in period depends on the individual. With this type of orientation, the child is much more likely to approach daily separations positively.

Watch the child to find her interests. Have these available when she arrives and gently try to engage her in activities. During initial contacts with a child, avoid quick movements and physical contact (unless the child requests it). Play next to this child. Describe what you are doing but do not expect a response. Try sharing a material with her without talking. Follow the

On his first day of preschool, Seng, a four-year-old boy for whom English is his second language, slumped against the door. He cried and called out to his father in his native language. The teacher cautiously approached with a clipboard and drawing paper. She drew a picture of a boy who was crying. Then a picture of a clock showing dismissal time and dad arriving. Next she drew the boy with a happy face. The teacher went on to draw a family and house. Seng named his family members and corrected the drawing so it depicted his family. The teacher handed him the clipboard and marker. She stayed with him while he drew.

Before too long the teacher announced, "In five minutes we'll go see what toys there are." When the time came to tour the room, Seng refused. The teacher took the drawing things and began to draw and label the toys in the room. Just minutes later, they were moving around the room together. The teacher showed him a pictorial schedule of their day and explained again when his father would return. Seng began to play with a toy that caught his eye. Before long other children joined him. Another child was overheard saying, "Don't worry. Your dad will be back soon. It will go fast. I promise."

child's lead in play. Let her direct you verbally or with her actions.

If the child is crying, reflect what she might be feeling. Say, "It's sad when Mom has to go." Reassure her that her parent(s) will return. Sing, "My mommy comes back, she always comes back to get me" (from the *Baby Songs* video; see Bibliography at the back of this book). Do a puppet play in which the puppet is frightened by being in the early childhood setting. Show how the provider can help the puppet meet others and find things to do. Make a pictorial schedule. Talk about what will take place when the child is with you so she doesn't have any misconceptions. Talk about the specific time someone will pick up the child (for example, after snack time or after games). Allow her to carry a security item such as a blanket, a cuddly toy, or a picture of her family.

Plan fun activities in which the child can succeed. Assign another child to the newcomer to act as a buddy and help her through routines. Recognize times she is actively engaged in play or with friends and whisper affirming messages such as, "Helen likes playing with you." Some children who feel they can't stop their parents from leaving try to control other things. They may hoard toys or insist on a certain chair. Understand the underlying need to "hold on" while gently introducing the concept of sharing toys with others.

➤ *Does the child become fussy at naptime or mealtime?*

Naptime and mealtime can remind a child of home. At naptime a child might miss reading a book or cuddling with a parent. Find out the family's naptime routine and repeat as much of it as possible. Encourage the child to bring a familiar blanket or cuddly animal. Play quiet, soothing music to provide a distraction as well as help to create atmosphere. Consider if the child is over tired from first exposures to a group setting. If so, allow additional rest periods earlier in the day or move naptime ahead a few minutes. Perhaps this child does not nap at home and is upset by the request. Strike a compromise such as a short rest time or time to read books. At mealtime, plan meals that are familiar to the child and include food she likes. Explain any mealtime routines. Encourage the child to eat without forcing (she may be too nervous to eat much).

➤ *Has the child been in your program for some time and is now tearful or upset at drop off?*

Look to see if there is a pattern to the upsets (for example, every Monday after a terrific weekend at home). Use appropriate suggestions listed under the first question above. Build your relationship with the child. Greet her daily. Find something special to share, such as a joke, a way she can help, or a common interest. Consider other sources of anxiety. Has there been a change at home or in the early childhood setting? Was there an upset with another child or adult? Is she upset because she was disciplined for something? Has a special friend or provider left the program? Support this child as she learns to cope with changes and her feelings.

➤ *Does this child fully engage in program activities?*

Although the child may not cry or show signs of anxiousness, the work of separation is not complete until she is fully engaged in the early childhood program. Watch to see that this child is participating and not just going through the motions until it is time to go home. Identify if this child has any favorite activities. Affirm her involvement in these by saying, "It's fun to paint at school" or "You really listened to story today." Preview things to look forward to the next day. Say, "Next time you come we'll read the book you were looking at." Be sure you do.

➤ *Is leaving the early childhood setting or the reunion with the parent difficult?*

Some children have so much fun or are so involved in activities that when their parent arrives to pick them up they cry or behave inappropriately. Warn the child her parent will be arriving soon. Wait until after this child leaves to start an involved or lengthy activity. Assure the child the toys will be available to play with next time. Encourage the parent(s) to allow enough time for pickup in case the child needs to finish a project or game. Reduce the amount of time spent in conversation between the adults so the parent can focus on the child. Share necessary information in writing or over the phone. Be clear who is responsible for guiding the child's behavior at pickup time. Sometimes each adult is waiting for the other to do something.

Work with the Parent(s)

As you talk with a family interested in your program, let them know of the phase-in period. Encourage them to spend time easing their child into your setting even if they think their child will be all right. Talk with parent(s) about how important it is to prepare their child for coming to your program. Give them the information for parent(s). Discuss the Plan for Action. When the child is attending, let the parent know of progress made toward independence. Reassure them that you are doing everything you can to help their child feel comfortable in your setting.

When to Get Help

If a child attends your program sporadically or is shy in all settings, separation may be an issue for a long time. A child who attends your program regularly for three to four months and still cries for long periods each time may need additional help. For a child experiencing this type of distress, suggest that the family talk with a parent educator or counselor who specializes in working with families of young children.

For Further Reading

Brenner, Barbara. *The Preschool Handbook.* New York: Pantheon Books, 1990.

Garber, Stephen, Marianne Garber, and Robyn Spizman. *Monsters Under the Bed and Other Childhood Fears*. New York: Villard Books, 1993.

I hate to leave Anna when she's crying. I feel so guilty but I have to get to work. Each time it happens I'm torn about what to do.

What Is It?

One of a child's first experiences separating from her parent comes when someone else cares for her. Fear of being separated can be stressful for the child whether the separation is for a short or a long period. Children periodically experience developmental peaks in separation anxiety. A number of these peaks take place during the infant and toddler years. This chapter focuses on preschool-aged children. For information on how to help infants and toddlers develop healthy attachments to others and cope with separation issues, read *Working and Caring* by T. Berry Brazelton (Addison-Wesley, 1985), and other similar references.

Most likely all preschool-aged children experience some feelings of separation anxiety. The degree to which your child shows her feelings will vary depending on her personality and previous experiences with separation. She may approach a new setting enthusiastically, seemingly unaffected by the separation. She may become upset, cry, or cling to you when it is time for you to leave. Or she may withdraw and refuse to engage in activities or talk. Helping an anxious child deal with her feelings is an important step in guiding her toward independence.

Observe and Problem Solve

Ask the following questions as you watch your child's responses to new providers. The suggestions will help you formulate a plan to ease your child's concerns and help her build healthy attachments.

➤ *Does your child become upset, cry, or fuss when she is left with a new provider?*

This is a normal reaction to being left the first few times. Ease your child into the program before beginning with the normal schedule. Ask for an orientation and phase-in period where you and your child visit the program. (If you aren't available, perhaps a grandparent or other trusted adult could substitute.) The first visit can be quite short. On following days, you and your child can attend together and gradually lengthen your stay. You can play near your child at first, then move to the side of the room to serve as a safe base from which to operate. Once your child seems comfortable, you can say good-bye and take a short walk or read a book in the car. The length of time spent away from your child can be increased each time until she is able to stay for the whole program day. With this type of orientation, your child is much more likely to approach daily separations positively.

There is a natural tendency to avoid something about which you are fearful. Decrease the amount of fear your child may be experiencing by getting as much information about the new setting as possible. Prepare your child by reading books and talking to others who attend. Pretend about going to this program. Use some of the words that are used, such as "snack time," "group time," and "free play." Take turns being the one who leaves and the one who is left behind. Accept your child's fear about being left with someone else but don't cater to it. Overprotecting your child from their fear may be natural, but could lead a child to think they have reason to be afraid. Be honest about your own feelings about leaving your child but be careful those feelings don't rub off.

When you and your child are at home and relaxed, create a positive mental image of the new setting. Emphasize that you will be back. Talk about things that may take place and how your child will fit in. Answer any "what if" questions your child may have in the best way that you can or promise to find out. Find another child going to the same program and get together a few times to help provide an acquaintance. Talk with your provider about letting your child carry a security item such as a cuddly toy, a blanket, or a picture of your family.

It is best to say good-bye before leaving rather than sneaking out, even if the child becomes upset. Sneaking out teaches the child to be wary about when you may leave. Once you say good-bye, leave promptly. The provider will do whatever can be done to help your child get involved and make a positive adjustment. You can call later for assurance that your child has settled down. Most often your child will shut off the tears and begin to play happily soon after you close the door.

➤ *Has your child been in the same program for some time and is now tearful or upset at drop off?*

Her anxiousness could be a delayed reaction to separation. Look to see if there is a pattern to the upsets (for example, every Monday after a terrific weekend). Use appropriate suggestions listed under the first question above. Consider other sources of anxiety. Has there been a change at home or in the early childhood setting? Was there an upset with another child or adult? Is she upset because she was disciplined for something? Is there an issue over naptime? Has a special friend or provider left the program? Support your child as she learns to cope with changes or with her feelings. Spend time before drop-off together. Create a routine around leaving the house and returning. Plan what you will do together when you get home.

➤ *Is leaving the early childhood setting or your return at the end of the day difficult?*

Some children have so much fun and are so involved in activities that when their parent arrives to pick them up they cry or behave inappropriately. Let your child know when you will be arriving. Let her know that you want her to put things away and get ready to leave when you get there. Call ahead if you are going to be unusually early or late so your provider can prepare your child. Empathize with how difficult it is to leave when the other children are still playing. Remind her of the plans you made to do something together once you return home and stick to them. Assure your child the toys will be available to play with next time. Allow enough time for pickup in case your child needs to finish a project or game. Reduce the amount of time spent in conversation with the adults so you can focus on your child. Share necessary information in writing or over the phone. Be clear who is responsible for guiding the child's behavior at pickup time. Sometimes each adult is waiting for the other to do something. If there is still difficulty, you may need to say, "Do you want to come now or in two minutes?" An alternative choice is "You can come by yourself or I will carry you."

Work with Your Provider

Ease your child into a new setting even if you think she may be all right. Once your child is attending on her own, ask your provider about progress made toward independence.

When to Get Help

If your child attends the program sporadically or is shy in all settings, separation may be an issue for a long time. Talk with a parent educator or counselor who specializes in working with families of young children if your child is still experiencing distress after attending the same program regularly for three to four months.

For Further Reading

Brenner, Barbara. *The Preschool Handbook.* New York: Pantheon Books, 1990.

Garber, Stephen, Marianne Garber, and Robyn Spizman. *Monsters Under the Bed and Other Childhood Fears.* New York: Villard Books, 1993.

A Plan for Action

To develop your Plan for Action, choose a goal that best fits your situation. Then determine three or four actions providers and parent(s) will take. Choose additional actions specific to the early childhood setting and home. Mark your choices on this summary or write them on the planning form that follows.

Sample goals for a child having difficulty with separation:
- Separates without upset.
- Leaves child care without protest.
- Engages in _____ and _____ each day (list an activity or two).
- Settles in to naptime or rest time without crying.
- Joins in conversation at snack or mealtime.
- Add your ideas.

Sample actions parent(s) and provider can take:
- Participate in a phase-in period.
- Accept this child's fear.
- Consider other sources of anxiety.
- Reassure this child her parent(s) will return.
- Reduce adult conversation at pickup time.
- Share necessary information in writing or on the phone
- Add your ideas.

Sample actions provider can take:
- Greet this child daily.
- Be responsible for behavior once this child enters.
- Allow a security item from home.
- Have activities of interest available when this child arrives.
- Offer foods this child likes to eat.
- Build relationship with this child.
- Play next to this child.
- Follow this child's lead in play.
- Avoid quick movements and physical touch (unless requested by the child).
- Reflect the feelings this child may be having.
- Put on a puppet play about separation.
- Assign another child as a buddy.
- Talk about the specific time this child will be picked up.
- Repeat as much of the family's naptime routine as possible.
- Compromise about the need for nap or the length of rest time.
- Do not start an involved or lengthy activity just before this child is picked up.
- Add your ideas.

Sample actions parent(s) can take:
- Pretend about going to your early childhood program.
- Spend time with your child prior to drop off.
- Bring a security item.
- Create routine around leaving and returning.
- Plan what you will do together when you get home.
- Say good-bye before leaving, then leave promptly.
- Allow adequate time for pickup.
- Be responsible for behavior whenever you are with the child.
- Talk with a parent educator or counselor. Share pertinent information with your provider.
- Add your ideas.

Parent(s) and Provider Action Form

Date:_____

Our plan for _____

    (CHILD'S NAME)

Goal

Write a realistic goal for this child using one of the examples from this chapter or one of your own.

_____

_____

_____

_____

Actions parent(s) and provider will take

Choose from those in this chapter or use your own ideas.

1. _____
2. _____
3. _____
4. _____

Actions provider will take

Choose from those in this chapter or use your own ideas.

1. _____
2. _____

Actions parent(s) will take

Choose from those in this chapter or use your own ideas.

1. _____
2. _____

We will check in to discuss progress or modify our plan on_____
(set a day six weeks to three months from now).

Signed

_____

(provider)

_____

(parent)

CHAPTER 2

No More Diapers: Toilet Training

Almost all the kids in my group are starting to use the toilet. There's only one boy who isn't getting it. He just doesn't seem interested. None of the normal encouragement that I give seems to work with him.

What Is It?

Becoming independent in toileting is a complex task. A child can be considered completely toilet trained when he is able to anticipate the urge to use the toilet, get there in time, pull down his pants, use the toilet, pull up his pants, and wash up after himself. For many, this is a complicated process that takes time to learn.

Observe and Problem Solve

It is important to consider many factors as you begin to teach a child to use the toilet. Use the following questions to help you prepare for this task.

➤ *Is this child ready?*

There are many pressures to begin training a young child. Probably the greatest pressure for a provider who changes a number of diapers in a day is that you are tired of changing diapers! Another reason may be the parent(s) want to get the process started. Regardless of these pressures, base your decision to begin toilet training on a child's readiness. When approached at the right time, toilet training can go quickly and easily. The average age a child is toilet trained falls between two-and-a-half and

three years of age for daytime dryness and between three and four years for nighttime. It is not unusual for some boys to be trained even later than this. Sometime after a child's second birthday, begin to watch for the following readiness signs:

• Wants to imitate and please adults.
• Understands and follows simple directions.
• Stays dry for longer and longer periods.
• Seems aware of urination and bowel movements.
• Prefers to be clean and dry.
• Tries to pull pants up and down.

➤ *Is this child showing an interest in using the toilet but not yet ready in other ways? Does he accompany others into the bathroom? Does he want to flush the toilet?*

If so, let this child see other young children use the toilet. Allow him to get used to the equipment by flushing or sitting on the stool. Talk with the child about "peeing" or "pooping," using whatever words you and the parent(s) have chosen. Avoid words such as "dirty" or "icky" to describe this natural function. When changing a diaper you can say, "You pooped. Let's get you cleaned up. It feels good to be all clean." When a child is learning about these sensations, he first recognizes that he is wet or soiled. Later, he begins to recognize when he is wetting. Finally, he learns he is about to wet.

➤ *Is it time to begin toilet training?*

Once you and the parent(s) have determined this child is ready to begin to use the toilet and you have done some of the things described above, be ready to make a concentrated effort for at least three to four weeks. Take this child to the bathroom after meals, after waking, and periodically throughout the day. Stay with him, singing songs or reading books so that he will consider going to the bathroom a positive time. If there are no results within five minutes, praise his effort and comment that maybe next time the "pee will come out." After several successes, switch to training pants. Help him remember to stop play long enough to use the bathroom.

If toilet training is unsuccessful after a reasonable period of time, try talking with the parent(s). Perhaps it would be best to let a few months pass before trying again. Delaying toilet training isn't a signal of failure but a signal that the child needs a little more time to develop the necessary muscle control.

Experts disagree about the toilet training diapers currently on the market (Pull Ups, for example). Some say they are merely a bigger-sized diaper. These people argue that a child needs to feel wet in order to prefer using the toilet. Other people say these have helped in making a smooth transition from diapers to independent use of the toilet. In some situations, these products may offer a compromise for parent(s) and providers.

➤ Does this child have accidents?

Even when a child is using the toilet a number of times per day, accidents are common and should be treated in a matter-of-fact manner. Clean up and change clothes. Encourage the child to use the toilet to empty his bladder. Support him by saying, "Accidents happen. Next time we'll have to stop playing earlier and get to the bathroom on time." Sometimes a child may be trained for a number of months and then have a series of accidents. If the accidents take place for more than a week, try to determine if the child is worried about something or if there is a medical reason for the setback. Offer the worried child your support. Get appropriate medical care for the child who needs it.

➤ Does this child seem to resist using the toilet?

Many children resist adult requests during their toddler and early preschool years. If this child is still in this stage, you may want to delay your plans to begin training until he is less resistant and more interested in learning to do this "grown-up" thing by himself. With a resistant child, it may help to say, "Let's go to the bathroom" rather than asking if he has to go (he is likely to answer "*No!*"). Give him the choice to use the potty chair or the big toilet. Simplify your directions so that you are sure he understands. A child may resist using the toilet because he is afraid of the flushing noise. If so, wait until the child has left the room before flushing. A child may fear falling in. Use a potty chair, a toilet seat adapter, or step stool to help him feel more secure. If this child is afraid that something will bite his bottom, you may have to convincingly call the culprit out of the toilet and order it out of your bathroom never to return again!

➤ Does this child seem to need an incentive to get the behavior started?

Some people prefer not to offer an incentive for a behavior that is so natural. Others find it very helpful in getting toilet training started. If you decide to use an incentive program, use gentle praise along with any trinket. Remember that the greatest incentive should be staying clean and dry. Incentive ideas include stickers, a star on the calendar, pennies in a piggy bank, barrettes and bracelets, or small cars. Be clear that when your supply is gone, he won't need any more because by then he'll know how to use the toilet. When the "goodies" are gone, involve him in another activity as soon as he is done so he won't notice the lack of a trinket.

Work with the Parent(s)

It is important that you and the parent(s) agree that it is time to begin toilet training. Sometimes a parent is anxious to begin the process. Other times the provider is ready to get started. Avoid requiring a child be trained for your convenience. This denies the individual the opportunity to get ready at his own pace. It may also lead the child and parent(s) to become anxious over this developmental milestone. Review the signs of readiness and decide together if the child is ready. When he is ready, use the Plan for Action to discuss how to proceed. Consistency between your approaches is especially important for the child in this complex learning process.

When to Get Help

A health care provider should see the child if he experiences any of the following difficulties: pain or burning during urination, weak or small stream of urine, consistently damp underwear, or persistent symptoms of diarrhea or constipation.

For Further Reading

Beebe, Brook McKamy. *Tips For Toddlers*. New York: Dell Publishing, 1983.

Galinsky, Ellen, and Judy David. *The Preschool Years*. New York: Times Books, 1988.

Lansky, Vicki. *Toilet Training*. Toronto: Bantam Books, 1984.

Joshua isn't at all interested in using the toilet. Other children his age are learning. One woman said her boy, who is the same age, was trained months ago!

What Is It?

Becoming independent in toileting is a complex task. A child can be considered completely toilet trained when he is able to anticipate the urge to use the toilet, get there in time, pull down his pants, use the toilet, pull up his pants, and wash up after himself. For many, this is a complicated process that takes time to learn.

Observe and Problem Solve

It is important to consider many factors as you begin to teach your child to use the toilet. Use the following questions to help you prepare for this task.

➤ *Is your child ready?*

There are many pressures to begin toilet training a young child. Other people may put pressure on you, your early childhood program may encourage it, or you may be tired of changing diapers and wish to be done with the expense of diapers. Regardless of these pressures, base your decision on your child's readiness. When approached at the right time, toilet training can go quickly and easily. The average age a child is toilet trained falls between two-and-a-half and three years for daytime dryness and between three and four years for nighttime. It is not unusual for some boys to be trained even later than this. Sometime after your child's second birthday, begin to watch for the following readiness signs:

• Wants to imitate and please parent(s).

• Understands and follows simple directions.

• Stays dry for longer and longer periods.

• Seems aware of urination and bowel movements.

• Prefers to be clean and dry.

• Tries to pull pants up and down.

➤ *Is your child showing an interest in using the toilet but not yet ready in other ways? Does your child follow you into the bathroom? Does he want to flush the toilet for you?*

If so, let your child see you use the toilet. Allow him to get used to the equipment by flushing for you or sitting on the stool. Decide what terms you will use to talk about urinating and defecating. You will probably want to use the same words used at your early childhood program. Talk with your child about "peeing" or "pooping," using whatever words you have chosen. Avoid words such as "dirty" or "icky" to describe this natural function. When changing a diaper you can say, "You pooped. Let's get you cleaned up. It feels good to be all clean." When a child is learning about these sensations, he first recognizes that he is wet or soiled. Later he begins to recognize when he is wetting. Finally he learns he is about to wet.

➤ *Is it time to begin toilet training?*

Once you have determined your child is ready to begin to use the toilet and you have done some of the things described above, you will need to make a concentrated effort for at least three to four weeks. Wait to train your child when there aren't a lot of other things going on such as a new baby or extended visit from grandparents. Dress your child in pants that are easy to pull up and down. Take your child to the bathroom after meals, after waking, and periodically throughout the day. Stay with him, singing songs or reading books so that he will consider going to the bathroom a positive time. If there are no results within five minutes, praise the effort and comment that maybe next time the "pee will come out." After several successes, switch to training pants. Help your child remember to stop play long enough to use the bathroom.

If toilet training is unsuccessful after a reasonable period of time, let a few months pass before trying again. Delaying toilet training isn't a signal of failure but a signal that your child needs a little more time to develop the necessary muscle control.

Experts disagree about the toilet training diapers currently on the market (Pull Ups, for example). Some say they are merely a bigger-sized diaper. These people argue that a child needs to feel wet in order to prefer using the toilet. Other people say these have helped in making a smooth transition from diapers to independent use of the toilet. In some situations, these products may offer a compromise for parent(s) and providers.

➤ Does your child have accidents?

Even when your child is using the toilet a number of times per day, accidents are common and should be treated in a matter-of-fact manner. Clean up and change clothes. Encourage your child to use the toilet to empty his bladder. Support him by saying, "Accidents happen. Next time we'll have to stop playing earlier to get to the bathroom on time." Sometimes a child may be trained for a number of months and then have a series of accidents. If the accidents take place for more than a week, try to determine if there is a medical reason for the setback or if the child is worried about something. Get appropriate medical care for your child if he needs it. Offer your worried child support. Spend extra time with him.

➤ Is your child resistant to using the toilet?

Many children resist adult requests during their toddler and early preschool years. If your child is still in this stage, you may want to delay your plans to begin training until he is less resistant to directions and more interested in learning to do this "grown-up" thing by himself. With a resistant child it may help to say, "Let's go to the bathroom" rather than asking if he has to go (he is likely to answer "No!"). Give him the choice to use the potty chair or the big toilet. Simplify your directions so that you are sure he understands. A child may resist using the toilet because he is afraid of the flushing noise. If so, wait until the child has left the room before flushing. A child may fear falling in. Use a potty chair, a toilet seat adapter, or step stool to help him feel more secure. If your child is afraid that

something will bite his bottom, you may have to convincingly call the culprit out of the toilet and order it out of your bathroom never to return again!

➤ Does your child seem to need an incentive to get the behavior started?

Some people prefer not to offer an incentive for a behavior that is so natural. Others find it very helpful in getting toilet training started. If you decide to use an incentive program, use gentle praise along with any trinket. Remember that the greatest incentive should be staying clean and dry. Incentive ideas include stickers, a star on the calendar, pennies in a piggy bank, barrettes and bracelets, or small cars. Be clear that when your supply is gone, he won't need any more because by then he'll know how to use the toilet. When the "goodies" are gone, involve him in another activity as soon as he is done, so he won't notice the lack of a trinket as much.

➤ Is your child using the toilet during the day but unable to stay dry at night?

Nighttime dryness lags behind daytime by a number of months for many children and by years for some. Nighttime wetting is not usually considered a problem until a child is six or seven years old. To make it as easy as possible for the child to use the bathroom at night, keep the house warm, dress him in pajamas that are easy to remove, light the way to the bathroom, and willingly accompany him if he calls out to you. Experts disagree about restricting the child's fluid intake in the evening. Some say this tends to focus the child on wanting a drink and makes him more anxious. There is also controversy about waking a child to take him to the bathroom before the parent(s) go to bed. Opponents argue that this doesn't teach the child to respond to their physical signals. Regardless of your approach, make up your child's bed with two sets of sheets and waterproof pads to make nighttime accidents easier to clean up. If needed, you can strip one set and the next is already in place.

Work with Your Provider

It is important that you and your provider decide together that it is time to begin toilet training. Sometimes a parent is anxious to begin the process. Other times the provider (who changes diapers of your child and others all day) is ready to get started. Review the signs of readiness and decide together if your child is ready. Talk with your provider about how to proceed. Consistency between your approaches is especially important for your child in this complex learning process.

When to Get Help

Take your child in for a medical examine if he experiences any of the following difficulties: pain or burning during urination, weak or small stream of urine, consistently damp underwear, or persistent symptoms of diarrhea or constipation.

For Further Reading

Beebe, Brook McKamy. *Tips For Toddlers*. New York: Dell Publishing, 1983.

Galinsky, Ellen, and Judy David. *The Preschool Years*. New York: Times Books, 1988.

Lansky, Vicki. *Toilet Training*. Toronto: Bantam Books, 1984.

A Plan for Action

To develop your Plan for Action, choose a goal that best fits your situation. Then determine three or four actions providers and parent(s) will take. Choose additional actions specific to the early childhood setting and home. Mark your choices on this summary or write them on the planning form that follows.

Sample goals for a child learning to use the toilet independently:
- Shows an interest in toileting.
- Tells an adult when he is urinating.
- Tells an adult just before he needs to use the toilet.
- Uses the toilet with minimal help from an adult.
- Add your ideas.

Sample actions parent(s) and provider can take:
- Watch for signs of readiness.
- Let this child flush and sit on the toilet.
- Affirm "It feels good to be dry and clean."
- Take this child to the bathroom routinely.
- Give a direction to go to the bathroom. Say, "Let's go to the bathroom now."
- Give a resistant child the choice to use the big toilet or the potty chair.
- Praise efforts.
- Treat accidents in a matter-of-fact manner.
- Provide a small incentive.
- Add your ideas.

Sample actions provider can take:
- Let this child see other young children use the toilet.
- Add your ideas.

Sample actions parent(s) can take:
- Let this child see you use the toilet.
- Dress this child in clothes that are easy to pull up and down.
- Provide training pants and extra clothing.
- Take your child to see your health care provider if he is experiencing symptoms of a medical problem. Share pertinent information with your provider.
- Add your ideas.

Parent(s) and Provider Action Form

Date:_____

Our plan for _____
                 (CHILD'S NAME)

Goal

Write a realistic goal for this child using one of the examples from this chapter or one of your own.

_____

_____

_____

_____

Actions parent(s) and provider will take

Choose from those in this chapter or use your own ideas.

1. _____
2. _____
3. _____
4. _____

Actions provider will take

Choose from those in this chapter or use your own ideas.

1. _____
2. _____

Actions parent(s) will take

Choose from those in this chapter or use your own ideas.

1. _____
2. _____

We will check in to discuss progress or modify our plan on_____

(set a day six weeks to three months from now).

Signed

_____

(provider)

_____

(parent)

CHAPTER 3

I'm Not Eating That: Finicky Eating

Kaleigh would sit for hours staring at her food if I let her. She eats one or two bites but won't touch any more. I'm afraid she isn't eating enough.

What Is It?

Most children are picky about what they eat at some point and all children have likes and dislikes of their own. But some children seem to refuse most foods. A child who is picky may be one who reacts to changes in texture, temperature, or taste. That child may have food preferences that are different from those of the person responsible for preparing the food. Whatever the reason, finicky eating can be upsetting if it seems as if a child isn't eating enough. Poor eating habits can be the cause of other problems too. A child who is not well nourished may be tired, irritable, inattentive, or less social.

Observe and Problem Solve

You may need to watch this child's eating habits over a period of a few months to get a true picture of what is taking place. Keep records of the things you observe and your hunches about what it means. Ask the following questions to help you know what to look for and to think about solutions that fit your situation.

➤ *Does this child eat well at times?*

Eating patterns of young children can be sporadic. They may eat a lot one day and little the next; or they may eat ravenously for a month and then lose most of their appetite. Some children prefer one food for two or three weeks and then claim it's "yucky" the next time you offer it. Many children store up on calories before a growth spurt, growing out before they grow up. Healthy children can have very different calorie intake needs. Children are good at regulating the amount of food they need. Let the child decide how much to eat.

➤ *Are there certain foods (or food groups) this child prefers over others?*

We all prefer some foods to others. Children tend to prefer those with less pungent flavors. They have more taste buds in a more concentrated area so many foods are too strong for them. Keep this child's preferences in mind when you are planning your menu. Include in your menu at least one thing you know she likes and can fill up on at each meal. Avoid offering this child a special food that is not a part of the meal. This singles her out and can make her feel out of place. Accept a child's dislike of certain foods as a personal preference and don't force. Plan other foods that offer the same nutritional value.

New foods need to be introduced as many as ten times before a child considers them familiar and is likely to eat them. Offer a new food as an extra and ask that the child tries only a small taste.

Prepare foods in different ways. Vegetables can be eaten with dip, steamed, in soup, in a casserole, and with sauce or cheese. Brightly colored foods are eye-catching and more appealing.

➤ Is this child hungry?

A child's stomach is about the same size as her fist; as a result, she needs smaller amounts of food but more often throughout the day. Schedule snacks that are part of the child's daily nutrition plan midway between meals. Watch so the child does not fill up on water, milk, or juice just before or at the beginning of the meal. Try offering half of a serving of the beverage along with the meal and the other half at the end. Make sure the child has had an adequate amount of physical activity between each meal to burn off calories and increase her appetite for the next meal.

➤ Does this child play with her food by touching it or pushing it around on her plate?

Playing with food may suggest the child is full or uninterested in the serving. It may also be this child's way of exploring it visually and physically, as she does so many other things in her environment. Learning what foods are and how to feed yourself is a messy job. Expect messes as young children become proficient at learning to eat. Promote an understanding and interest in a food by asking children to help to grow it, pick it out in the grocery store, or prepare it. Preschool children can wash and scrub vegetables; open, pour, and stir mixes; tear lettuce; and peel fruits.

➤ Is this child too busy to eat?

When children are busy talking, playing, or watching television, they have difficulty concentrating on their meal. Establish mealtime routines and behavioral expectations. Warn children that mealtime is approaching so they have time to finish play or realize they must leave it for a short time. Engage children in a calming activity (such as looking at books, playing with playdough, or drawing) prior to meals so they come to the table relaxed. Sit with the children, carry on pleasant mealtime conversation, and model good manners.

If you are concerned that this child is taking an inordinate amount of time to complete a meal, you may need to set a reasonable amount of time (say 30 minutes), gently remind her to concentrate, warn her that in 5 minutes the meal will be over, then respectfully but firmly remove the food. If this child wants to finish well before the others, require that she stay at the table to converse for a minimum amount of time. After this period, she can be dismissed to a quiet activity that is not disturbing the other children's meal.

➤ Is this child begging for foods not offered?

Set limits about begging for things. Say, "We will be eating what is offered; I know there are things here you like and can fill up on." In the same way, set limits about commenting on their dislikes. Preferences can be stated in ways that do not offend the person who has worked hard to prepare the food. Teach children to say, "I don't care for that" or "No, thank you" rather than "I hate that." If others copy one child's negativism, take that child aside and come up with a secret signal (like tugging on her earlobe) that allows her to express her preferences but that does not upset others.

➤ Is this child expressing her independence at the table as well as in other areas of her life?

Young children are looking for ways they can express their independence and individuality. Preschool-aged children love to be offered choices. Whenever possible, avoid power struggles about food. Instead, offer healthy choices by saying, "Would you like Cheerios or Rice Krispies cereal for breakfast?" Avoid rules such as finishing everything on your plate. Encourage her to try one taste of everything. You can control what the child is offered, but the child controls how much she will eat. Encourage the child to eat until she has satisfied her hunger. Avoid using desserts or sweets as a reward. Offering dessert as a reward implies that it is better than the rest of the foods offered. Make dessert nutritious so it can be part of the meal.

Work with the Parent(s)

When a child is not eating well, parents understandably become worried about their child's health and nutrition. Well-meaning people may begin to push food or get into power struggles over food issues. Set guidelines for your food program in your policies. Consider including something such as, "Good nutritious foods will be offered; the child will be allowed to control how much of each food will be eaten; manners and appropriate mealtime behaviors will be taught; the individual feeding preferences that require substitute menu items must be provided and prepared by the parent." Use the Plan for Action to discuss how you will work with a child who is a finicky eater. Establish consistency between home and the early childhood setting so the child will be clear about your expectations.

When to Get Help

If you are still concerned after observing this child's eating patterns for a number of months and trying the suggestions, consult with your food program representative or a nutritionist. The child's health care provider should be consulted if you believe she is significantly underweight.

For Further Reading

Berman, Christine, and Jacki Fromer. *Meals Without Squeals*. Palo Alto, CA: Bull Publishing, 1991.

Satter, Ellyn. *How to Get Your Kid to Eat... But Not Too Much*. Palo Alto, CA: Bull Publishing, 1987.

I get so frustrated with Kaleigh's picky eating. I just want her to eat one more bite!

What Is It?

Most children are picky about what they eat at some point and all children have likes and dislikes of their own. But some children seem to refuse most foods. A child who is picky may be one who reacts to changes in texture, temperature, or taste. That child may have food preferences that are different from those of the person responsible for preparing the food. Whatever the reason, parents can become concerned when it seems as if their child isn't eating enough.

Observe and Problem Solve

You may need to watch your child's eating habits over a period of a few months to get a true picture of what is taking place. Keep records of the things you observe and your hunches about what it means. Ask the following questions to help you know what to look for and to think about solutions that fit your situation.

➤ *Does your child eat well at times?*

Eating patterns of young children can be sporadic. They may eat a lot one day and little the next; or they may eat ravenously for a month and then lose most of their appetite. Some children prefer one food for two or three weeks and then claim it's "yucky" the next time you offer it. Many children store up on calories before a growth spurt, growing out before they grow up. Healthy children can have very different calorie intake needs. Children are good at regulating the amount of food they need. Let your child decide how much to eat.

➤ *Are there certain foods (or food groups) your child prefers over others?*

We all prefer some foods to others. Children tend to prefer those with less pungent flavors. They have more taste buds in a more concentrated area so many foods are too strong for them. Keep your child's preferences in mind when you are planning your family menu. Include at least one thing you know she likes and can fill up on at each meal. Avoid becoming a short order cook, however, cooking what each person requests. Accept your child's dislike of certain foods as a personal preference and don't force. Plan other foods that offer the same nutrition value.

New foods need to be introduced as many as ten times before a child considers them familiar and is likely to eat them. Offer a new food as an extra and ask that the child tries only a small taste.

Prepare foods in different ways. Vegetables can be eaten with dip, steamed, in soup, in a casserole, and with sauce or cheese. Brightly colored foods are eye-catching and more appealing.

➤ *Is your child hungry?*

A child's stomach is about the same size as her fist; as a result, she needs smaller amounts of food but more often throughout the day. Schedule snacks that are part of your child's daily nutrition plan midway between meals. Watch so your child does not fill up on water, milk, or juice just before a meal or at the beginning of the meal. Try offering half of a serving of the beverage along with the meal and the other half at the end. Make sure your child has had an adequate amount of physical activity between each meal to burn off calories and increase her appetite for the next meal.

➤ *Does your child play with her food by touching it or pushing it around on her plate?*

Playing with food may suggest the child is full or uninterested in the serving. It may also be your child's way of exploring it visually and physically, as she does with many other things in her environment. Learning what foods are and how to feed yourself is a messy job. Expect messes as young children become proficient at learning to eat. Promote an understanding and interest in a food by asking your child to help to grow it, pick it out in the grocery store, or prepare it. Preschool children can wash and scrub vegetables; open, pour, and stir mixes; tear lettuce; and peel fruits.

➤ *Is your child too busy to eat?*

When children are busy talking, playing, or watching television, they have difficulty concentrating on their meal. Establish mealtime routines and behavioral expectations. Warn your child that mealtime is approaching so she has time to finish her play or to realize she must leave it for a time. Try to engage your child in a calming activity (such as looking at books, playing with playdough, or drawing) prior to meals so she comes to the table relaxed. Sit with your child, carry on pleasant mealtime conversation, and model good manners.

If your child is taking an inordinate amount of time to complete a meal, you may need to set a reasonable amount of time (say 30 minutes), gently remind her to concentrate, warn her that in 5 minutes the meal will be over, then respectfully but firmly remove the food. If she wants to run off to play before giving much attention to her meal, require that she stay at the table to converse with the family for a minimum amount of time. She may eat more just because it is in front of her.

➤ *Is your child begging for foods not offered?*

Set limits about begging for things. Say, "We will be eating what is offered; I know there are things here you like and can fill up on." In the same way, set limits about commenting on your child's dislikes. Preferences can be stated in ways that do not offend the person who has worked hard to prepare the food. Teach your child to say, "I don't care for that" or "No, thank you" rather than "I hate that."

➤ *Is your child expressing her independence at the table as well as in other areas of her life?*

Young children are looking for ways they can express their independence and individuality. Whenever possible, avoid power struggles about food. Offer healthy choices by saying, "Would you like Cheerios or Rice Krispies cereal for breakfast?" Avoid rules such as finishing everything on your plate. Encourage her to try one taste of everything. You can control what the child is offered, but the child controls how much she will eat. Encourage your child to eat until she has satisfied her hunger. Avoid using desserts or sweets as a reward. Offering dessert as a reward implies that it is better than the rest of the foods offered. If you believe there is a problem with your child's nutrition, make dessert nutritious so it can be a part of the meal.

Work with Your Provider

Providers do their best to offer nutritious foods that children like. Many of them work with food programs that help to monitor their menu planning and provide them with consultation about recipes and meals that appeal to young children. They are working hard to promote healthy eating habits and appropriate mealtime behaviors. If a special diet is essential, you may need to provide and prepare the food. If you must make menu substitutions, keep the substitute items similar to what the rest of the children are eating. Eating things that are very different can make your child feel out of place. Meet with your provider to discuss what steps you will take in working with a child who is finicky. Establish consistency between home and the early childhood setting so your child will be clear about expectations.

When to Get Help

If you are still concerned after observing your child's eating patterns for a number of months and trying the suggestions, consult your health care provider. Your health care provider can tell you if your child is growing and developing at an appropriate rate.

For Further Reading

Berman, Christine, and Jacki Fromer. *Meals Without Squeals*. Palo Alto, CA: Bull Publishing, 1991.

Satter, Ellyn. *How to Get Your Kid to Eat... But Not Too Much*. Palo Alto, CA: Bull Publishing, 1987.

A Plan for Action

To develop your Plan for Action, choose a goal that best fits your situation. Then determine three or four actions providers and parent(s) will take. Choose additional actions specific to the early childhood setting and home. Mark your choices on this summary or write them on the planning form that follows.

Sample goals for a child who is a finicky eater:
- Tries one bite of foods offered.
- Makes a choice when offered two healthy alternatives.
- Focuses attention on eating during meals.
- Sits with the group/family for _____ minutes at mealtime (choose a time that is slightly more than this child's current performance).
- Add your ideas.

Sample actions parent(s) and provider can take:
- Establish mealtime routines.
- Sit with this child during mealtimes and try to make them a pleasant experience.
- Let this child decide how much to eat.
- Offer at least one thing this child likes and can fill up on at each meal.
- Avoid power struggles that force an amount.
- Encourage this child to take one taste of foods offered.
- Offer new foods as extras.
- Offer adequate physical activity between meals.
- Involve this child in preparation whenever possible.
- Offer half the beverage serving along with the meal and half at the end.
- If this child dawdles, set a reasonable amount of time to eat before removing the food.

- If this child rushes through a meal, require that she stay at the table for a minimum of time.
- Teach this child to say "No, thank you" as a way to state her preference.
- Add your ideas.

Sample actions provider can take:
- Dismiss children who finish early to a quiet activity that will not distract others from mealtime.
- Consult with a nutritionist or food program representative. Share pertinent information with the parent(s).
- Add your ideas.

Sample actions parent(s) can take:
- Substitute different foods with the same nutrition value.
- Offer healthy choices.
- Set limits about begging for things not offered at meal.
- Take your child to see your health care provider if your child is significantly underweight. Share pertinent information with your provider.
- Add your ideas.

Parent(s) and Provider Action Form

Date:_____

Our plan for _____
            (CHILD'S NAME)

Goal

Write a realistic goal for this child using one of the examples from this chapter or one of your own.

_____

_____

_____

_____

Actions parent(s) and provider will take

Choose from those in this chapter or use your own ideas.

1. _____
2. _____
3. _____
4. _____

Actions provider will take

Choose from those in this chapter or use your own ideas.

1. _____
2. _____

Actions parent(s) will take

Choose from those in this chapter or use your own ideas.

1. _____
2. _____

We will check in to discuss progress or modify our plan on_____

(set a day six weeks to three months from now).

Signed

_____

(provider)

_____

(parent)

CHAPTER 4

Let's Go, Go, Go: Activity Level

FOR PROVIDERS

Tony comes in running and doesn't stop. He wiggles and bothers others while I try to read a story. He never really finishes anything during free play. I need to take vitamins just to keep up.

What Is It?

Children grow increasingly active until three to four years of age when their activity level peaks. This activity level means most children won't attend to any one thing for very long periods of time. Depending upon the activity, a two-year-old child is generally able to sit and attend for two to three minutes and a five-year-old child for fifteen to twenty minutes. The wonderful amount of energy that children possess becomes problematic when a child is unable to focus attention long enough to learn from an activity. Children with high activity levels may be easily distracted, have trouble finishing projects, and act without considering the consequences of their behavior. Because a child who is always on the move tends to hear a number of messages about his behavior, it is especially important to protect his self-esteem while helping him learn to focus his energy.

Observe and Problem Solve

Observe and record the length of time this child is able to attend to activities of choice, adult-directed activities, and play with others. Pick another child about the same age and temperament and record his attention span for similar activities. Compare their records and use this information to gain perspective, identify trouble spots during the day, and consider influences on activity level. Your observations and the suggestions that follow may give you insights as to how to work with this child.

➤ *What types of materials hold this child's interest?*

More than likely, this child will be drawn to materials and activities that allow him to move. Let this child release energy by getting outside at least one time each day. Provide many ways for him to move indoors too. Include large muscle equipment such as an indoor climbing structure, rocking boat, or a "Sit and Spin" as regular pieces in your environment. Plan additional movement activities such as throwing foam balls into a basket, jumping across a tape mark on the floor, dropping pegs into a plastic jar, carrying cotton balls on a spoon, or dancing to music. To help calm or soothe the active child, offer sensory activities such as pouring sand, water, or cornmeal and manipulating playdough. As you learn this child's other interests, be sure to include them in your environment too.

➤ *During free play does this child go from toy to toy without playing with anything?*

Consider your environment and how it may affect the child's activity level. Make sure activities are simple enough for him to be successful and yet difficult enough to challenge him. Plan traffic patterns so others are not walking through his play and distracting him. Arrange your space so quiet activities are not right next to loud ones. Eliminate runways or wide open spaces that invite running. Consider the overall

Indoor Large Muscle Activity Ideas

1. Tape a rope on the floor or use chalk to draw a squiggly design. Children walk in the circles or jump from opening to opening.

2. Throw bean bags into boxes, baskets, or hoops. Place the targets on the floor, chair, or shelf to change the angle of the toss.

3. Keep balloons in the air by bouncing them off your head, elbow, knee, or hands. Strengthen the balloons by placing one inside another before blowing them up. (Do not let children put balloons by their mouths. Be careful to get all the pieces of broken balloons thrown away so children cannot swallow them.)

4. Suspend a balloon from the ceiling (using a double-strength balloon will make the game last longer). Use a rolled-up newspaper to bat at it.

5. Pretend to go skating by placing each foot in a shoe box or box top and sliding around the room.

6. Tape a rope on the floor in a straight line or use tape to mark a line on the floor. Children walk across it trying to balance as they go.

7. Make a hopscotch pattern on the floor with tape or chalk. Let children use a checker or coin to mark their spot.

8. Straddle a stick horse or yardstick and gallop around a track. To avoid crashes, establish a direction for all horse riders to follow.

9. Make stretch ropes. You'll need 1 1/4 inch elastic (24 inches per rope), scissors, needle and thread. Sew each piece of elastic into a circle. Children place their feet on the elastic and hold on to the other side of the circle with their hands. They can jump or hop around the room. They can strengthen their arm muscles by stretching the rope in all directions with their hands. (Do not allow children to place these stretch ropes around their necks.)

10. Use an old pillowcase as a jumping bag. Set up chairs or cones for the jumpers to hop around. Time the children for added fun; have them try to improve upon their own best time.

noise level. Reduce noise by adding materials that absorb it or teaching children to use quieter voices. Look at your space to see if it might be over stimulating. Cut back on the number of materials available at one time and rotate them. Reduce the decorations or displays on the wall without making things look sterile. Display toys and materials attractively so that it is easier to see what is available and to make choices.

Ask this child to choose what he will play with. Stay with him while he gets started. If he begins to wander without purpose, go to him and ask him what he will do next. Be sure to notice and comment on his behavior when he is engaged in an activity. Commenting when he is successfully involved gives him attention for the behavior you are looking for. Determine if he is wandering because others are excluding him from play. If so, see chapter 11, "I Want to Play Too: Joining a Group of Players."

➤ *Does this child have difficulty changing from one activity to the next?*

Children who have high activity levels seem to do best with predictable schedules and routines. Pay attention to the rhythm of your day. Pattern your schedule so that opportunities to move come before and after activities that require the child to sit. Provide a balance between adult-directed and child-directed activities. Make a pictorial schedule of your day and teach children what comes next.

Give a warning a few minutes before an activity comes to an end. Be specific about what this child is to do and where he is to go during changes in activity. Tell him to stand by his cubbyhole, sit on his carpet square, or line up at the back door. Fill waiting times by having this child as a helper, singing songs, or doing slow repetitive actions to help everyone relax.

➤ *Does this child have difficulty sitting in a group to listen to a story? Does he leave the group or fidget inattentively? Does he pester others by talking to them or touching them?*

Consider alternative activities this child (and others) might do while some are listening to the story. Perhaps looking at picture books independently, stringing beads, or playing with playdough could be offered as choices. Motivate this child to join the group by more fully engaging him. Sing songs, do finger plays, put on puppet plays, act out stories, or tell flannelboard stories. Pique the interest of this child by beginning the group activity with a short demonstration, using a prop, wearing a costume, or posing a riddle or mystery question. Keep group times short. Plan a seating arrangement that places the active child in the center of the back. There he can see well, but won't block the view of others if he is wiggly. Place children who are able to ignore him on either side of him. Mark his spot with tape or a carpet square. Talk about personal space as if it is a bubble that surrounds each person. During group, children are to keep their hands and feet inside their bubble. Reinforce this child for looking at you and participating in the activity by giving him the thumbs up or okay signal. When you do need to draw his attention to the activity, touch him gently or ask him a multiple choice question. Say something like, "Do you think the boy in the story will run home or run to school? Let's find out." This way he has a chance to respond correctly.

➤ *Does this child act impulsively, without considering the consequences of his behavior?*

Teach this child to control his actions. Play stop-and-freeze games where the child stops in response to a drum, bell, or word from you. Practice many times so that he learns to stop when you call his name. When he is having difficulty, move close to him. Confidentially state the rule. For example, you might say, "It's not okay to open the guinea pig's cage. What can you do instead?" Provide alternative actions from which he can choose. If needed, offer choices such as, "You can open and close the doors on this shape box or draw a picture of the guinea pig." At other times, play "What if" games with this child. Ask, "What if you were playing with a toy car and someone else came along and took it?" Brainstorm appropriate solutions to each situation posed. Evaluate the solutions and choose the one that would be best.

If his impulsive behavior upsets another child, help him focus his attention on the response he receives. Say, "Look at Tyrone's face. He is really sad." Work with him to problem solve how he might help Tyrone feel better. In other situations, this child may not understand the unintentional behaviors of others. For instance, if he is in a crowded space and someone accidentally pushes him, he may think he was attacked. His natural response might be to defend himself. Teach him to recognize the push as accidental and say, "That's okay" or "No problem."

Work with the Parent(s)

Share with this child's parent(s) examples of what he is interested in, his strengths, and the steps you are taking to build on those. Arrange a meeting to discuss difficult situations. Use the Plan for Action that follows to determine the steps that will be taken at home and in the early childhood setting. Establishing consistency will help this child learn adaptive behaviors more quickly.

When to Get Help

It is sometimes difficult to determine when a child with a high activity level is outside of the norm. Put the suggestions into action for three to four months. Then consider if the child is still in constant motion; has difficulty sticking to an activity for more than a few minutes; acts without considering the consequences; or continues to have difficulty following routines. If needed, suggest that the parent(s) contact resources in your community that may be of help. These may include the child's health care provider, an early childhood education or assessment program, or a family counselor specializing in working with young children.

For Further Reading

Budd, Linda. *Living With the Active Alert Child*. Seattle: Parenting Press, 1993.

Cherry, Clare. *Think of Something Quiet*. Carthage, IL: Fearon Teacher Aids, 1981.

Johnson, Dorothy Davies. *I Can't Sit Still*. Santa Cruz, CA: ETR Associates, 1992.

Torbert, Marianne, and Lynne Schneider. *Follow Me Too*. Reading, MA: Addison-Wesley Publishing, 1993.

Tony has been on the move since he was tiny. He's up at dawn, busy all day, and doesn't seem tired by bedtime. He's very interested in things he sees but doesn't stay with any one thing for very long. We've always had a hard time keeping up with him.

What Is It?

Children grow increasingly active until three to four years of age when their activity level peaks. This activity level means most children won't attend to any one thing for very long periods of time. Depending upon the activity, a two-year-old child is generally able to sit and attend for two to three minutes and a five-year-old child for fifteen to twenty minutes. The wonderful amount of energy that children possess becomes problematic when a child is unable to focus attention long enough to learn from an activity. Children with high activity levels may be easily distracted, have trouble finishing projects, and act without considering the consequences of their behavior. Because a child who is always on the move tends to hear a number of messages about his behavior, it is especially important to protect his self-esteem while helping him learn to focus his energy.

Observe and Problem Solve

Observe and record the length of time your child is able to attend to activities of choice, adult-directed activities, and play with others. Visit your early childhood program and observe another child about the same age and with a similar temperament. Record this child's attention span for similar activities. Compare their records and use this information to gain perspective. Your observations and the suggestions that follow may give you insights as to how to help your child.

➤ *What types of materials hold your child's interest?*

More than likely, your active child will be drawn to materials and activities that allow him to move. Let your child release energy by getting outside at least one time each day. Don't rely on your early childhood program to provide all the outdoor opportunities he needs. Provide many ways for him to move indoors too. Have equipment such as a mini-trampoline, indoor climbing structure, or a "Sit and Spin" as regular pieces in your home. Allow additional activities such as throwing foam balls into a basket, jumping across a tape mark on the floor, dropping pegs into a plastic jar, carrying cotton balls on a spoon, or dancing to music. Plan additional activities such as swimming, skating, and playing at neighborhood playgrounds to help meet his need to move. To help your child calm down or relax, offer sensory activities such as pouring sand, water, or cornmeal and manipulating playdough.

➤ *Does your child go from toy to toy without playing with anything?*

Consider your home and how it may affect your child's activity level. Make sure activities are simple enough for him to be successful and yet difficult enough to challenge him. Look at his room and play areas to see if they might be over stimulating. Cut back on the number of materials available at one time and rotate them. Reduce the number of decorations or displays on the wall without making things look sterile. Display toys and materials attractively so that it is easier to see what is available and to make choices.

Ask your child to choose what he will do when he is to play alone. Stay with him while he gets started. If he begins to wander without purpose, go to him and ask him what he will do next. Be sure to notice and comment on his behavior when he is engaged in an activity. Commenting when he is successfully involved gives him attention for the behavior you are looking for.

➤ *Does your child have difficulty changing from one activity to the next?*

Children who have high activity levels seem to do best with predictable schedules and routines. Pay attention to the rhythm of your day. Pattern your schedule so that opportunities to move come before and after activities that require your child to sit. Provide a balance between adult-directed and child-directed activities.

Give a warning a few minutes before an activity comes to an end. Be specific about what your child is to do as you change activities. For example, tell him to wait for you at the back door. Plan your outings thoughtfully. If you must take an active child to the store, it is best to do it on a day when he is more cooperative. Carry some things with you that will help to occupy him if you must wait at a restaurant or the doctor's office.

➤ *Does your child have difficulty sitting to listen to a story?*

Consider ways to more fully engage your restless child in this type of activity. Read books that allow him to touch, pat, or open flaps; tell stories with puppets or act out stories. Pique your child's interest in the book by asking questions as you read or trying to correctly predict the end of the story. Keep story times short so they will be enjoyable for you and your child. Read in a place where there are few distractions and he can focus on the book. Tell him when he is being a good listener.

➤ *Does your child act impulsively, without considering the consequences of his behavior?*

Teach your child to control his actions. Play stop-and-freeze games where your child stops in response to a whistle, bell, or word from you. Practice many times so that he learns to stop when you call his name. When he is having difficulty during play, move close to him. Give him a confidential message about his behavior. For example, you might say, "It's not okay to open the guinea pig cage. What can you do instead?" Provide alternative actions from which he can choose. If needed, offer choices such as "You can open and close the doors on this shape box or draw a picture of the guinea pig." At other times play "What if" games with your child. Ask, "What if you were playing with a toy car and someone else came along and took it?" Brainstorm appropriate solutions to each situation posed. Evaluate the solutions and choose the one that would be best.

If his impulsive behavior upsets another person, help him focus his attention on the response he receives. Say, "Look at Tyrone's face. He is really sad." Work with him to problem solve how he might help Tyrone feel better. In other situations, your child may not understand the unintentional behaviors of others. For instance, if he is playing with others and someone accidentally pushes him, he may think he was attacked. His natural response might be to defend himself. Teach him to recognize the push as accidental and say, "That's okay" or "No problem."

➤ *Does your child seem to get more energetic when you would expect him to be exhausted?*

Children who are active may not look as if they need sleep, but they do. Your child may have difficulty calming down and stopping play long enough to go to sleep. Develop a consistent bedtime routine to help him know it is time to stop and unwind. Include changing clothes, a healthy snack, brushing teeth, and reading or telling a story, then into bed. If your child protests, separate sleep time from bedtime by saying, "You don't have to go to sleep right away but you must lie quietly in your bed." Bedtime itself should be at approximately the same time each night. It is tempting to keep a child who is active up a few minutes later, thinking he will sleep in the next day. Most often this backfires and the child is up at the same time or earlier. Generally, children will fall asleep fairly soon when they have had a busy day, when bedtime comes at a reasonable time, and when there is a consistent routine.

Work with Your Provider

Caring for a child who is active at home offers unique challenges as does caring for this child in a group setting. Listen to your provider's concerns and do what you can to make sure your child has plenty of opportunity to move, eat a balanced diet, and get adequate rest. Work with your provider to determine what additional steps will be taken at home and in the early childhood setting. Establishing consistency between settings will help your child learn adaptive behaviors more quickly.

When to Get Help

It is sometimes difficult to determine when a child with a high activity level is outside of the norm. Put the suggestions into action for three to four months. Then consider if your child is still in constant motion; has difficulty sticking to an activity for more than a few minutes; acts without considering the consequences; or continues to have difficulty following routines. If needed, contact resources in your community that may be of help. These may include your child's health care provider, an early childhood education or assessment program, or a family counselor specializing in working with young children.

For Further Reading

Budd, Linda. *Living With the Active Alert Child.* Seattle: Parenting Press, 1993.

Cherry, Clare. *Think of Something Quiet.* Carthage, IL: Fearon Teacher Aids, 1981.

Johnson, Dorothy Davies. *I Can't Sit Still.* Santa Cruz, CA: ETR Associates, 1992.

Torbert, Marianne, and Lynne Schneider. *Follow Me Too.* Reading, MA: Addison-Wesley Publishing, 1993.

A Plan for Action

To develop your Plan for Action, choose a goal that best fits your situation. Then determine three or four actions providers and parent(s) will take. Choose additional actions specific to the early childhood setting and home. Mark your choices on this summary or write them on the planning form that follows.

Sample goals for a child with a high activity level:

- Engages in activities of choice for _____ minutes (choose a time that is slightly more than this child's current performance).
- Sits at snack or a short group activity for _____ minutes (choose a time that is slightly more than this child's current performance).
- Moves from one activity to the next independently.
- Attends to short, interactive group time.
- Stops actions when an adult calls his name.
- Add your ideas.

Sample actions parent(s) and provider can take:

- Take this child outside at least one time each day.
- Provide indoor movement activities.
- Offer sensory activities.
- Cut back on the number of materials available and rotate them.
- Display materials and toys so choices are easier to make.
- Notice and comment on this child's behavior when he is engaged in an activity.
- Sandwich a passive activity between two that allow this child to move.
- Be specific about behavioral expectations during changes in activities.
- Move close to this child or whisper when you need to talk to him about his behavior.
- Play "What if" games to help this child learn consequences of his actions.
- Help this child focus on the responses of others to his behaviors.
- Teach him to recognize accidents.
- Add your ideas.

Sample actions provider can take:

- Plan things that especially interest this child.
- Reduce waiting times; fill those that cannot be eliminated.
- Plan traffic patterns to reduce disruption and runways.
- Help this child make activity choices during free play.
- Stay with this child while he gets started in an activity.
- Watch to see if this child is excluded from play by others.
- Keep group time short.
- Start group with an attention grabber.
- Place this child where he can see and hear well at group.
- Mark this child's spot with tape or carpet square.
- Teach this child about personal space.
- Reinforce this child for paying attention to the group activity.
- Regain this child's attention with a touch or a multiple choice question.
- Add your ideas.

Sample actions parent(s) can take:

- Offer balanced meals.
- Make sure this child gets adequate rest.
- Develop a consistent bedtime routine.
- Encourage an interest in reading.
- Tell this child when he is being a good listener.
- Take things for this child to do on outings when he may need to wait.
- Consult with another professional regarding your child's activity level (for example, health care provider, early childhood assessment program, or family counselor).
- Add your ideas.

Parent(s) and Provider Action Form

Date:_____

Our plan for _____
         (CHILD'S NAME)

Goal

Write a realistic goal for this child using one of the examples from this chapter or one of your own.

_____

_____

_____

_____

Actions parent(s) and provider will take

Choose from those in this chapter or use your own ideas.

1. _____
2. _____
3. _____
4. _____

Actions provider will take

Choose from those in this chapter or use your own ideas.

1. _____
2. _____

Actions parent(s) will take

Choose from those in this chapter or use your own ideas.

1. _____
2. _____

We will check in to discuss progress or modify our plan on_____
(set a day six weeks to three months from now).

Signed

_____

(provider)

_____

(parent)

CHAPTER 5

Watch This! Attention Getting

Tia wants me to watch her every move. When I spend time with her it never seems to be enough. I feel like she demands so much attention that I don't have enough time for the other children.

What Is It?

Everyone wants attention. Children like to have adults spend time with them, notice the things they are doing, and comment on what they are learning. Some children seem to require more attention than others and some seem to have an insatiable need for attention. In working with a child that requires a high level of attention, recognize the important role providers play in the development of the child's self-esteem. It is easy to tire of their pleas to play with you or watch them, yet it is essential to respond in a supportive manner. At the same time, you can help them take steps toward independence.

Observe and Problem Solve

Watch this child to see under what circumstances she needs attention. Your answers to the following questions will help as you develop a Plan for Action.

➤ *Does this child call your attention to her activities?*

"Watch this," "Watch me," and "Look" are favorite phrases of a child who is excited about new-found skills. Take pleasure in the learning that is taking place. Help this child feel good about her accomplishments by commenting,

"I bet it feels good to make it all the way to the top of the climber." Comment on specifics in her artwork. Say, "Look how you swirled the purple paint" or "I see colorful lines and circles." Help her find pleasure in her own work by asking, "What do you like best about it?" or "Which part did you work on the hardest?" Set limits on how many times you will watch her. Say, "I will watch you one more time then I must watch one of the other children."

➤ *Does this child ask you to play with her all the time?*

Make sure materials are displayed at a child's level so she can help herself and play independently. Check to see if toys and materials are at an appropriate level of difficulty for this child. If she seems bored, add toys and materials that are more difficult or that she hasn't seen in some time. Get out easier toys for the child who may feel she cannot do the activities available to her. Structure the day so that there are group activities and independent playtimes.

Spend time with this child early in the day to meet some of her needs for attention. Make it clear how long you will play with her. Draw the play session to an end after five to ten minutes. Promise to play with her again later or the next day. Once your time together is over, explain in a kind but firm way that you have other things you must do and that she must do something on her own. Help her decide what activity she will engage in and get her started. When she is playing alone, look for a break or pause in the action. Comment on her independence or about how busy she is. Be careful not to unnecessarily interrupt. Arrange times when you work side by side. Set her up with an activity next to you. Continue with your work while she does hers. Your nearness will help her feel valued.

➤ *Does this child brag or exaggerate in order to get your attention?*

If so, the child may be trying to gain recognition or favor. Help her feel proud and competent in many areas. Bolster her confidence by commenting on times when she is strong, making good decisions, or running fast, for example. De-emphasize competition. Notice when she tries her best. Play cooperative games. Plan activities in which children work together, such as making a fruit salad or telling a group story.

➤ *Does this child interrupt or ask questions frequently?*

Make a rule for all children that only one person talks at a time. Explain, confidentially, to this child that she needs to respect the person who is speaking and wait her turn. Tell her, "I'd like to hear what you have to say but someone else is talking. You need to wait until they are done." Ask her to tell you one word so you can both remember what she has to tell you. Then she must wait. Be sure to ask her about it at an appropriate time. If she interrupts frequently during group time, talk with her about being quiet. Give this child the thumbs up or okay signal when she is doing a good job, as a way to attend to her without interrupting the activity.

➤ *Does this child look at you and then break a rule?*

This child may have learned the only time she gets attention is if she is being reprimanded for doing something wrong. Pay attention to this child early in the day and often when she is behaving appropriately. Let her know you appreciate her hard work to follow the rules. Teach her words to use to ask you to pay attention to her. She can say, "Sit by me" or "Hold my hand." When she learns some simple phrases, she may not need to seek your attention inappropriately as often.

When she does break a rule, pay as little attention as possible. State simply what has been done that is not acceptable, then move her to another part of the room or require her to choose a quiet activity for a short time. Do not engage in discussion or argue with this child at this point. Her arguing may be an attempt to keep you in-

volved with her. Instead, let her know what she must do before you will attend to her again. For instance, you might say, "I will come and sit by you when you have stopped kicking the table." If this child is imitating inappropriate behaviors of others, let her know she has good ideas of her own and doesn't need to copy other people.

➤ *Does it seem as if this child is never satisfied with the amount of attention she receives?*

This child may finish reading books with you for over ten minutes and then ask you to play a game with her. She may have difficulty playing alone or may not have satisfying peer relationships. Observe to see if this child has good peer interaction skills. If not, use the suggestions in chapter 11, "I Want to Play Too: Joining a Group of Players." Be firm but fair regarding the amount of time you have to spend with her. Spend time with this child before she searches for ways (that may be inappropriate) to get your attention. Arrange a short break for yourself each day by planning independent play activities or asking someone to cover for you.

Work with the Parent(s)

Let the parent(s) know that this child requires a great deal of attention in the group setting. Find out if there have been any changes or problems recently that lead the child to seek adult support. Work with the parent(s) to develop a Plan for Action. Establishing consistency between home and the early childhood setting will help this child toward independence.

When to Get Help

By attending to a child many times a day and letting her know when her behavior is appropriate, most children will have their needs for attention met. However, if a child does things for attention that are dangerous or self-injuring, refer the family to a counselor who specializes in working with young children.

For Further Reading

Budd, Linda. *Living with the Active Alert Child.* Seattle: Parenting Press: 1993.
Sobel, Jeffrey. *Everybody Wins: 393 Non-Competitive Games for Young Children.* New York: Walker and Company, 1983.

Tia wants me to play with her all the time. I never get a break. I'm lucky if I get to go to the bathroom by myself.

What Is It?

Everyone wants attention. Children like to have adults spend time with them, notice the things they are doing, and comment on all they are learning. Some children require more attention than others and some seem to have an insatiable need for attention. In living with a child that requires a high level of attention, recognize the important role you play in the development of their self-esteem. It is easy to tire of your child's pleas to play with you or to watch them, yet it is essential to respond in a supportive manner. At the same time, you can help them take steps toward independence.

Observe and Problem Solve

Watch your child to see under what circumstances she needs attention. Your answers to the following questions will help as you decide how to teach her to be more independent.

➤ *Does your child call your attention to her activities?*

"Watch this," "Watch me," and "Look" are favorite phrases of a child who is excited about new-found skills. Take pleasure in the learning that is taking place. Help your child feel good about her accomplishments by commenting, "I bet it feels good to make it all the way to the top of the climber." Comment on specifics in things she does. Say, "Look how you swirled the purple paint" or "You lined up all your stuffed animals when you cleaned." Help her find pleasure in her own work by asking, "Which part did you work on the hardest?" Set limits on how many times you will watch her. Say, "I will watch you one more time then I must do something else."

➤ *Does your child ask you to play with her all the time?*

Make sure materials are available to her so she can help herself and play independently. Check to see if toys and materials are at an appropriate level of difficulty. If she seems bored, add some that are more difficult or that she hasn't seen in some time. Get out easier toys for her if she feels she cannot do the activities. Structure your day so that you alternate between doing things together and independent playtime.

Spend time with your child early in the day to meet some of her needs for attention. Make it clear how long you will play with her. Draw the play session to an end after five to ten minutes. Promise to play again later. Once your time together is over, explain in a kind but firm way that you have other things you must do and that she must do something on her own. Help her decide what activity she will engage in and get her started. When she is playing alone, look for a break or pause in the action. Comment on her independence or about how busy she is. Be careful not to unnecessarily interrupt. Arrange times when you work side by side. Set her up with an activity next to you. Continue with your work while she does hers. Your nearness will help her feel valued.

➤ *Does your child brag or exaggerate in order to get your attention?*

If so, she may be trying to gain recognition or favor. Help her feel proud and competent in many areas. Bolster her confidence by commenting on times when she is strong, making good decisions, or running fast, for example. De-emphasize competition. Notice when she tries her best. Plan activities in which you work cooperatively, like making a fruit salad or getting the house cleaned.

➤ *Does your child interrupt or ask questions frequently?*

Make a rule that only one person talks at a time. Explain to your child that she needs to respect the person who is speaking and wait her turn. Tell her, "I'd like to hear what you have to say but someone else is talking. You need to wait until they are done." Ask her to tell you one word so you can both remember what she has to tell you. Then she must wait. Be sure to ask her about it at an appropriate time.

➤ *Does your child look at you and then break a rule?*

Your child may have learned the only time she gets attention is if she is being reprimanded for doing something wrong. Pay attention to your child early in the day and often when she is behaving appropriately. Let her know you appreciate her hard work to follow the rules. Teach her words to use to ask you to pay attention to her. She can say, "Sit by me" or "Hold my hand." When she learns some simple phrases, she may not need to seek your attention inappropriately as often.

When she does break a rule, pay as little attention as possible. State simply what has been done that is not acceptable, then move her to another part of the room or require her to choose a quiet activity for a short time. Do not engage in discussion or argue with your child at this point. Her arguing may be an attempt to keep you involved with her. Instead, let her know what she must do before you will attend to her again. For instance, you might say, "I will come and sit by you when you have stopped kicking the table."

➤ *Does it seem as if your child is never satisfied with the amount of attention she receives?*

You may finish reading books for over ten minutes with your child and then she asks you to play a game with her. Be firm but fair regarding the amount of time you have to spend with her. Spend time before she searches for ways (that may be inappropriate) to get your attention. Arrange a short break for yourself each day. Provide lots of stimulating activities for your child. Explain this will be your alone time. She is to play by herself until alone time is over. Start with a very short time (only two or three minutes to begin with). Gradually increase the length of time. (Appropriate expectations might be: five minutes for a three year old, ten minutes for a four year old, and fifteen minutes for a five year old.)

Work with Your Provider

You know how difficult it can be to provide your child with the amount of attention she requires at home. A provider has as many demands on her time and usually more children vying for attention. Support your provider by spending time with your child before and after the early childhood program she attends. Meet with your provider to discuss what steps you will take. Establishing consistency between home and the early childhood setting will help your child toward independence.

Corrina knew from the time Grace was little that she needed more attention than Corrina's other children. In fact, Grace demanded more attention. After struggling for years to keep up with the demand, Corrina decided to institute a new plan. At the same time each day Grace would have "quiet time," a time when she would play by herself. Together Corrina and Grace decorated a box and gathered toys that Grace was to use only during quiet time. They put in the box magnetic letters and shapes and a cookie sheet to put them on; a puppet; books; large wooden beads to string; a yarn ball to toss; and tapes for her tape recorder.

Each day Corrina and Grace went to Grace's room and got down the special box. They put a tape on the recorder and set the timer so they would know when quiet time was over. Corrina left the room and closed the door behind her. At first quiet time lasted only four minutes. Even though it was only four minutes, it was four minutes of quiet. Corrina knew the idea wouldn't work if Grace had to go much longer. Once the timer rang, Corrina returned to Grace's room. Often the room was in a shambles but Corrina wanted to make sure she appreciated Grace for playing alone during quiet time. So they read a book or played a game before tackling the mess. As Grace's attention span lengthened, quiet time lengthened too. Eventually, Grace was able to give her mom a 15-minute break.

When to Get Help

By attending to a child many times a day and letting her know when her behavior is appropriate, most children will have their needs for attention met. However, if your child does things for attention that are dangerous or self-injuring, talk to a counselor who specializes in working with young children.

For Further Reading

Budd, Linda. *Living with the Active Alert Child.* Seattle: Parenting Press: 1993.

Sobel, Jeffrey. *Everybody Wins: 393 Non-Competitive Games for Young Children.* New York: Walker and Company, 1983.

A Plan for Action

To develop your Plan for Action, choose a goal that best fits your situation. Then determine three or four actions providers and parent(s) will take. Choose additional actions specific to the early childhood setting and home. Mark your choices on this summary or write them on the planning form that follows.

Sample goals for a child requiring a high level of attention:
- Compliments her own work.
- Plays alone for _____ minutes each day (choose a time that is slightly more than her current performance).
- Waits to talk until it is her turn.
- Asks for attention in appropriate ways.
- Add your ideas.

Sample actions parent(s) and provider can take:
- Arrange toys and materials so the child can help herself.
- Spend time one on one with this child early in the day and often.
- Firmly draw a play session to a close.
- Comment on this child's independence.
- Be specific as you comment about this child's work.
- Ask this child to praise herself.
- Pay attention to this child with nonverbal signals when you can't talk with her.
- Set limits on how many times you will watch this child.
- Arrange times to work side by side.
- Make it clear that only one person is to talk at a time.
- Pay little attention to this child when she breaks a rule.
- Restate the rule that has been broken and tell this child her behavior is unacceptable.
- Move this child to another part of the room and ask her to choose a quiet activity for a short time.
- Arrange a short break for yourself each day.
- Add your ideas.

Sample actions provider can take:
- Alternate group activities and independent playtimes.
- De-emphasize competition.
- Add your ideas.

Sample actions parent(s) can take:
- Alternate between doing things together and independently.
- Plan cooperative activities.
- Talk with a counselor if your child does things that are extremely dangerous or self-injuring. Share pertinent information with your provider.
- Add your ideas.

Parent(s) and Provider Action Form

Date:_____

Our plan for _____
                    (CHILD'S NAME)

Goal

Write a realistic goal for this child using one of the examples from this chapter or one of your own.

_____

_____

_____

_____

Actions parent(s) and provider will take

Choose from those in this chapter or use your own ideas.

1. _____
2. _____
3. _____
4. _____

Actions provider will take

Choose from those in this chapter or use your own ideas.

1. _____
2. _____

Actions parent(s) will take

Choose from those in this chapter or use your own ideas.

1. _____
2. _____

We will check in to discuss progress or modify our plan on_____

(set a day six weeks to three months from now).

Signed

_____

(provider)

_____

(parent)

CHAPTER 6

Want to Play Doctor? Sexual Curiosity

FOR PROVIDERS

One day I found three of the kids behind a chair in the living room checking out each other's body parts. I told them they needed to put their clothes on and come do something with me in the kitchen. I was so surprised I'm not sure I responded in the best way.

What Is It?

Sexual curiosity and behaviors of young children range from questioning to "playing doctor" to imitating adult sexual behavior. Providers may be concerned by any of these behaviors if they are caught off guard or unprepared to respond. Your responses must be based on knowledge of your program's policies, licensing policies, the social climate of your community, parent requests, and accurate information about the sexual development of young children. Most important in responding to a child's questions is to convey an acceptance of their curiosity.

Observe and Problem Solve

Consider the following questions as you prepare to respond.

➤ *Does the child ask questions about body parts, reproduction, or intimacy?*

Let the child know that his question is an important one. Then follow established policy by either referring the question back to the child's parent(s) or answering honestly. Use accurate information and the appropriate terminology.

The use of nicknames may lead to confusion. When talking about body parts, for example, use "penis," "scrotum," "vulva," "vagina," and "breast." Keep your answers to questions simple. Answer only what the child is asking without providing more information than the child is asking or for which he is ready. Keep the lines of communication open so that the child knows you are approachable for future discussion.

➤ *Does the child "play doctor" or curiously look at other children's genitals?*

Most children are curious about the differences between boys' and girls' bodies. They need to know that boys have penises and girls have vulvae. Boys and girls are different and each is special in their own way. If children "play doctor," accept their curiosity as natural and calmly redirect to other activities. You might say, "I need you to keep your clothes on. Genitals are private and clothes keep them covered."

➤ *Does the child masturbate during naptime or as a self-comfort activity?*

Some children have learned to comfort themselves by manipulating their genitals or rubbing themselves on a toy or bedding. When this is done on their cots or in a private manner, it rarely is a problem. If the child does this in front of others, acknowledge that he has found a way to feel good but limit it to a private time. Say something like, "You've found that feels good but I'd like you to wait until nap or when you're alone." Give the child other ways to comfort himself by allowing him to carry a cuddly toy. Or give him a way to work out some of his emotions by manipulating clay or other sensory materials.

➤ *Does the child use sexual behavior as an attention getter?*

Some children try to get attention by imitating kissing, flirting, or provocative dancing they have seen. They need to know that they can gain your attention in other ways. Give them attention many times per day when they are not behaving in this fashion. They may need simple messages like, "That looks like something a grown-up might do. Let's do something else instead."

➤ *Do children in your group know what to do if they are uncomfortable with the direction play is moving?*

Sexual play between two children of approximately the same age and size implies a certain level of consent among players. However, children need to know that if they are uncomfortable with play, they can say no; they can say, "I don't like that"; they can leave the area; they can tell a grown-up; or they can yell for help.

Work with the Parent(s)

It is especially important to communicate with parent(s) about their child's sexual curiosity. Let them know the kinds of questions their child is asking so they can prepare to answer the questions in their own way. Parents also have a right to know when their child is showing curiosity about other people's bodies and how you are handling this interest. If there is a concern about a child who has sophisticated knowledge, proceed with caution. Talk with the parent(s) if you feel the child's exposure to sexual information should be limited. Use the Plan for Action to decide what steps you will take in working with this child.

When to Get Help

Children are exposed to adult sexual behaviors through observing adults, advertising, and the media. Providers must determine if the child is aware of an unusually sophisticated level of sexual behavior or sexual activity. If so, it might suggest that the child has been or is being sexually abused. This is a serious situation that must be handled cautiously. It is important to document any behaviors of concern. Indicators of sexual abuse include but are not limited to the following:

- experiencing pain or soreness in the genital area when walking, sitting, urinating, or defecating
- demonstrating adult-like sexual behavior
- being fearful of adults or certain individuals
- extreme fear of certain places or situations
- talking about or drawing sexually advanced information or behavior.

One of these indicators alone is not likely to be enough information to be certain abuse is taking place. If you see a pattern of these behaviors or your concerns persist, it is important to take action. Many states require providers to report suspicions of child abuse, neglect, or sexual abuse. Even if your state does not mandate you to report, you have an ethical obligation to protect the child by describing your suspicions to the appropriate authorities. Report your concerns and let the authorities decide if there is adequate evidence to pursue an investigation. If they investigate, they will handle the discussion with the parent(s).

For Further Reading

Brick, Peggy, Sue Montfort, and Nancy Blume. *Healthy Foundations: The Teacher's Book.* Hackensack, NJ: The Center for Family Life Education, 1993.

Leight, L. *Raising Sexually Healthy Children.* New York: Rawson Associates, 1988.

Wilson, Pamela. *When Sex Is the Subject.* Santa Cruz, CA: Network Publications, 1991.

One morning as Samuel and I were rushing around getting ready for the day, he asked, "Mom, have you got a penis?" My mouth dropped open. I didn't know what or how much to say.

What Is It?

Sexual curiosity for preschool-aged children ranges from asking questions to taking an interest in their own bodies and those of others to imitating sexual behaviors they see. Their behaviors can catch a parent off guard and unprepared to handle certain situations. Reflect on the attitudes you want to convey before responding. Most important in responding to a child's questions is to convey an acceptance of their curiosity.

Observe and Problem Solve

Consider the following questions as you prepare to respond.

➤ *Does your child ask questions about body parts, reproduction, or intimacy?*

Most parents want to answer their child's questions honestly and openly. Some find this difficult and embarrassing, others think of it as another opportunity to teach their child about the wonders of life. As you answer, convey positive attitudes toward sex and intimacy as natural and wonderful human events. The attitudes you communicate may actually be more important than the explanation you give. When you respond to your child's questions, indicate your willingness to talk with him about his questions. Try to establish open lines of communication for further discussions. In your answers, be sure to use the correct terminology. The use of nicknames may lead to confusion. When talking about body parts, for example, use "penis," "scrotum," "vulva," "vagina," and "breast." Answer only what your child is asking without providing more information than he is asking or for which he is ready.

We were driving down the highway when my four-and-a-half-year-old daughter asked me, "Mom, when you had the baby did you have to take all your clothes off?" My mind raced as I thought, "Oh dear, here it comes! The big discussion about where babies come from." I grappled with what I would tell her. Then I remembered reading that less is better than more: Start with the simplest answer, then give more information if she continues to ask for it.

It seemed as if I had driven miles before I answered, "Yes, but I had hospital pajamas I could wear." I braced myself for the next question. Her response came, "Weren't you embarrassed?" I answered, "No, doctors see lots of bodies." To my surprise that was all she wanted to know. She changed the subject and I gratefully chatted with her about something else. At the same time, I thought I'd better prepare myself to handle her next questions with more grace and ease.

➤ *Does your child "play doctor" or curiously look at another's genitals?*

Most children are curious about boys' and girls', men's and women's bodies. They need to know that boys have penises and girls have vulvae. Boys and girls are the same in many ways but different too. Each is special in their own way. You may want to have appropriate books or anatomically correct dolls that help children learn about bodies. In order to keep children from exploring in ways that might hurt them, limit "doctor play." If you find children who have disrobed, accept their curiosity as natural. Say something like, "You need to keep your clothes on when you play. Genitals are private and clothes keep them covered." Redirect them to other types of doctor care or another activity.

➤ *Does your child masturbate or touch himself as a self-comforting activity?*

Some children have learned to comfort themselves by manipulating their genitals or rubbing themselves on a toy or bedding. When this is done in private, it rarely is a problem. If your child does this in front of others, acknowledge that he has found a way to feel good, but limit it to private time. Say something like, "You've found it feels good to touch yourself; I'd like you to do that in private."

➤ *Does your child use sexual behavior as an attention getter?*

Some children try to get attention by imitating the kissing, flirting, or provocative dancing they have seen. Your child needs to know that he can gain attention other ways. Give him attention many times per day when he is not behaving in this fashion. He may need simple messages like, "That looks like something grown-ups would do. Let's go do something else instead."

➤ *Does your child know what to do if he is uncomfortable with the direction play is moving?*

Sexual play between two children of approximately the same age and size implies a certain level of consent among players. However, your child needs to know that if he is uncomfortable with play, he can say no; he can say, "I don't like that"; he can leave the area; he can tell a grown-up; or he can yell for help.

Work with Your Provider

It is important to communicate with your provider about your child's sexual curiosity. Let her know, in general, the kinds of questions your child is asking so she can be prepared to respond. Make it clear if you prefer to answer your child's questions or if she may make use of the moment by answering honestly and accurately. If your child is curious about people's body parts or interested in sex play, ask the provider to supervise play closely. Talk with your provider to determine what steps you will take in working with your child.

When to Get Help

Children are exposed to adult sexual behaviors through observing adults, advertising, and the media. If your child seems to have an advanced understanding of sexual behavior or sexual information, you must determine how your child obtained it. If you think he is exposed to too much information through the media, limit his television and movie viewing.

There is little risk of your child being abused in an early childhood setting. However, if you believe your child could have only come to know sexual information by direct exposure to sexual activity, your child may have been or is being sexually abused. If so, he needs your protection. Indicators of sexual abuse include but are not limited to the following:

- experiencing pain or soreness in the genital area when walking, sitting, urinating, or defecating
- demonstrating adult-like sexual behavior
- being fearful of adults or certain individuals
- becoming extremely fearful of certain places or situations
- talking about or drawing sexually advanced information or behavior.

One of these indicators alone is not likely to be enough information to be certain abuse is taking place. If you see a pattern of these behaviors or your concerns persist, it is important to take action. Report your concerns to law enforcement or to child protection services. They can help you decide if there is adequate evidence to indicate abuse and where to go for further help. Do not delay. Your child's well-being depends on your action.

For Further Reading

Leight, L. *Raising Sexually Healthy Children.* New York: Rawson Associates, 1988.

Wilson, Pamela. *When Sex Is the Subject.* Santa Cruz, CA: Network Publications, 1991.

A Plan for Action

To develop your Plan for Action, choose a goal that best fits your situation. Then determine three or four actions providers and parent(s) will take. Choose additional actions specific to the early childhood setting and home. Mark your choices on this summary or write them on the planning form that follows.

Sample goals for a child who is acting on his sexual curiosity:
- Limits masturbation to naptime or in private.
- Seeks attention in appropriate, childlike ways.
- Chooses activities other than sex play.
- Add your ideas.

Sample actions parent(s) and provider can take:
- Affirm questions about sex and body parts are important.
- Convey positive attitudes about sexual curiosity as a natural part of growing up.
- Use appropriate terminology when talking about bodies and bodily functions.
- Require children to wear clothes when they are with others.
- Redirect sex play to other types of activities.
- Attend to this child many times per day when he is doing a variety of childlike activities.
- Ask this child to limit masturbation to naptime or alone time.
- Monitor behavior.
- Keep a log of sexual behaviors of concern.
- Consider indicators of sexual abuse.
- If evidence suggests this child has been abused, contact the appropriate authorities.
- Add your ideas.

Sample actions provider can take:
- Answer questions honestly and openly.
- Tell the parent what questions have been asked.
- Refer questions about sex to the parent.
- Redirect sex play to other types of activities.
- Ask this child to limit masturbation to naptime or alone time.
- Add your ideas.

Sample actions parent(s) can take:
- Answer questions about sex and body parts openly and honestly.
- Limit his exposure to media and sexual activity of adults.
- Add your ideas.

Parent(s) and Provider Action Form

Date:_____

Our plan for _____
         (CHILD'S NAME)

Goal

Write a realistic goal for this child using one of the examples from this chapter or one of your own.

_____
_____
_____
_____

Actions parent(s) and provider will take

Choose from those in this chapter or use your own ideas.

1. _____
2. _____
3. _____
4. _____

Actions provider will take

Choose from those in this chapter or use your own ideas.

1. _____
2. _____

Actions parent(s) will take

Choose from those in this chapter or use your own ideas.

1. _____
2. _____

We will check in to discuss progress or modify our plan on_____
(set a day six weeks to three months from now).

Signed

_____
(provider)

_____
(parent)

CHAPTER 7

I *Am* Telling the Truth: Tall Tales and Falsehoods

FOR PROVIDERS

Choua has been telling a lot of fibs lately. She really gets upset when I confront her about them and insists she is telling the truth. What if she gets into a habit of lying to people?

What Is It?

As children learn about right and wrong, their understanding of the importance of truthfulness develops. Most children tell tall tales and falsehoods at some time. When children tell stories that are improbable or attempt to mislead, it can be upsetting. It isn't until three-and-a-half or older that a child typically possesses the skills needed to intentionally deceive. In order to lie, a child must be able to act calmly, think quickly, and talk about the abstract. Occasional falsifying on the part of a preschool-aged child is neither an indication of a poor moral upbringing nor a predictor of later deceit. The falsehoods do, however, allow parents and providers an opportunity to teach about telling the truth.

Observe and Problem Solve

When you listen to the child's tales, consider the following questions and look for insights to her motives. Make educated guesses about what is taking place and use the suggestions provided to promote truthfulness.

➤ *Is this child's story partially true? Are the facts becoming confused and fanciful?*

Sometimes when young children tell about things that have taken place, they confuse what has really happened with something they heard about, saw on television, or wish would happen.

Young children have vivid imaginations. This child may be so involved in telling her story that she begins to believe it is true. Avoid a power struggle about whether or not the story is accurate. Understand the wish underlying her statements. Comment on how fun it would be if it were true. Appreciate this child's ability to tell enjoyable stories. Give her an acceptable opportunity to do creative storytelling. Ask her to tell you some stories and write them down or tape record them.

This child may also be working to understand the difference between real and pretend. Talk about the difference when you read books, play in the dramatic play area, or talk about things others say (for example, "Joshua said he is going to the moon"). Use magazine ads that depict outrageous untruths (like picturing someone riding a bike under water) to help a child begin to recognize what is real or pretend.

Along with teaching about real and pretend, teach the difference between the truth and something that is untrue. In *Teaching Your Children Values*, the authors suggest using a game to teach the concepts of telling the truth and lying (see "True or Untrue: A Game" pg. 69). Play at a time when you are not in an upsetting situation. In this game, describe a few things that are true and a few that are untrue. Start with simple things the child can actually see and end with behaviors. After each statement, the child decides if it is true or untrue. For example: My shoes are blue (true). The grass is purple (untrue). What if I eat all my lunch and then say I'm done (true)? What if I break a toy and say I didn't do it (untrue)?

Tell the child that when a person tells something that isn't true it is called a "lie." Discuss how important it is to tell the truth so people know what happened, so she can learn what to do next time, and so people can trust her.

➤ *Is this child describing her capabilities, powers, or strengths?*

If the child is boasting about her abilities untruthfully, she may be trying to gain recognition or favor. Help her feel proud and competent in many areas. Bolster her confidence by commenting on times when she is strong, making good decisions, or running fast, for example. If she brags about being the fastest runner (but actually she is quite awkward in her running), don't draw attention to the discrepancy. Encourage continued practice by saying, "You get faster every time you practice" or comment, "It's nice you want to be a really fast runner. Running is good exercise."

➤ *Does this child try to cover a mistake, avoid embarrassment, or preserve privacy by saying something that isn't true?*

Young children have a tendency to conceal the truth about a mistake or an embarrassing situation. Help the child be truthful by avoiding questions that will tempt her to lie. If she accidentally spills something, don't ask, "Did you spill this juice?" Instead try, "I see the juice is spilled. Please get a rag and wipe it up." Or in a conflict situation, rather than asking, "Did you take it from her?" say, "Tell me what happened in your argument." In other instances, a child may feel questions about home are intrusive and may not answer honestly. Unless you are concerned about the child's well-being, respect this right to family privacy.

➤ *Does this child distort reality in order to get what she wants?*

During this egocentric period of a young child's life, she might tell untruths in accordance with her own desires. If you ask, "Did you get everything cleaned up in the block area?" this child may tell you she did—especially if she wishes this were true so she could get on to the next activity. First, help her avoid the temptation to lie by saying, "Let's go see how you're doing clean-

ing up the blocks." Then work with her to decide how to get done quickly so she can go on to the next activity. For example, she could ask you to help if the job seems overwhelming or talk with other children about doing their fair share. This way she will learn she doesn't have to lie to get what she wants.

➤ *Is this child testing you to see if she can trick or tease you?*

If so, this child may be looking for some power or control over you and others. Consider if she has opportunities to make choices. Offer plenty of child-directed activities. This child may try to trick you into doing things for her that she is capable of doing herself. Be good natured, yet let her know you are on to her tricks; say, "I think you are fooling me." Children enjoy being able to pull one over on adults. This type of manipulation of the truth is generally not too serious at this age.

➤ *Is this child telling you something that isn't true in order to avoid punishment or an unpleasant activity?*

Many children lie because they are worried about how angry grown-ups will be or to avoid being punished for their misdeeds. Teach this child that you can be trusted to handle misbehavior with relative calm, and that your responses will be fair. In this way she will not fear your responses and will learn to respect you. Children feel more guilt and are less likely to lie to people they respect.

Let this child know you feel it is important to tell the truth. Be truthful yourself. Adults are often times unaware of how many times they unintentionally model lying. Adults exaggerate experiences the child knows are not true; or adults give excuses that are not true in order to avoid unpleasant situations. For example, an adult may say they liked lunch when the child knows it was mediocre at best. Children who are very literal in their interpretations may view this as an example of lying.

Much of a young child's misbehavior is impulsive. When she denies it, she may be worrying that if she did this "bad thing" she will be viewed as "bad." Reassure her that everyone makes mistakes. If she continues to deny something, consider that she may be telling you the truth. Demonstrate that you trust her by believing her. When she does tell the truth, label it as the truth (so she ties the word to her experiences). Let her know you appreciate it. Thank her for her honesty. When you know she has done something, you might say, "I see you ripped the poster when you were angry." If she denies it, call the argument to an end by saying, "I don't want to argue about lying." Focus instead on what can be done to make it right. Perhaps she will need to tape the ruined poster back together.

Work with the Parent(s)

Support parents who are trying to raise honest children by implementing the suggestions above. Work with them so their child will receive messages about the importance of truthfulness. When a child is consistently deceiving you, talk with the parent(s). Discuss situations that are recurring and develop a Plan for Action. Establishing consistency between home and the early childhood setting will help this child learn appropriate behaviors more quickly.

When to Get Help

Children who break rules, get caught, and fear punishment are likely to lie more frequently. Be sure that you teach children how to behave appropriately by guiding behavior rather than harsh discipline. If this child is fearful when discussing behavioral mistakes, document what this child says and does as well as your concerns. Talk with child protection services if you have reason to believe this child is lying to avoid abusive punishment. If this child lies each time she is in a stressful situation but you do not believe she is being mistreated, refer the family to a parent educator or counselor who specializes in working with young children.

For Further Reading

Ekman, Paul. *Why Kids Lie*. New York: Charles Scribner's Sons, 1989.

Eyre, Linda, and Richard Eyre. *Teaching Your Children Values*. New York: Simon & Schuster, 1993.

Kitzinger, Sheila, and Celia Kitzinger. *Tough Questions*. Boston: The Harvard Common Press, 1991.

I can't believe Choua will look right at me and say she is done brushing her teeth when she hasn't even been in the bathroom. If she lies at this age what will it be like when she is a teenager?

What Is It?

As children learn about right and wrong, their understanding of the importance of truthfulness develops. Most children tell tall tales and falsehoods at some time. When children tell stories that are improbable or attempt to mislead, it can be upsetting. It isn't until three-and-a-half or older that a child typically possesses the skills needed to intentionally deceive. In order to lie, a child must be able to act calmly, think quickly, and talk about the abstract. Occasional falsifying on the part of a preschool-aged child is neither an indication of a poor moral upbringing nor a predictor of later deceit. The falsehoods do, however, allow you an opportunity to teach about telling the truth.

Observe and Problem Solve

When you listen to your child's tales, consider the following questions and look for insights to her motives. Make educated guesses about what is taking place and use the suggestions provided to promote truthfulness.

➤ *Is your child's story partially true? Are the facts becoming confused and fanciful?*

Sometimes when young children tell about things that have taken place, they confuse what has really happened with something they heard about, saw on television, or wish would happen.

Your child's imagination is probably quite vivid and she may be so involved in telling her story that she begins to believe it is true. Avoid a power struggle about whether or not the story is accurate. Understand the wish underlying her statements. Comment on how fun it would be if it were true. Appreciate your child's ability to tell enjoyable stories. Give her an acceptable opportunity to do creative storytelling. Ask her to tell you some stories and write them down or tape record them.

Your child may also be working to understand the difference between real and pretend. Talk about the difference when you watch television, read books, or talk about things others say (for example, "Joshua said he is going to the moon").

Along with teaching about real and pretend, teach the difference between the truth and something that is untrue. In *Teaching Your Children Values*, the authors suggest that you use a game to teach the concept of telling the truth and lying (see "True or Untrue: A Game" pg. 69). Play at a time when you are not involved in an upsetting situation. In this game, describe a few things that are true and a few that are untrue. Start with simple things your child can actually see and end with behaviors. After each statement your child decides if it is true or untrue. For example: My shoes are blue (true). The grass is purple (untrue). What if I eat all my lunch and then say I'm done (true)? What if I break a toy and say I didn't do it (untrue)?

Tell your child that when a person tells something that isn't true it is called a "lie." Be clear that lying is wrong. Discuss how important it is to tell the truth so people know what happened, so she can learn what to do next time, and so people can trust her.

➤ *Is your child describing her capabilities, powers, or strengths?*

If your child is boasting about her abilities untruthfully, she may be trying to gain recognition or favor. Help your child feel proud and competent in many areas. Bolster her confidence by commenting on times when she is strong, making good decisions, or running fast, for example. If she brags about being the fastest runner (but actually she is quite awkward in her running), don't draw attention to the discrepancy. Encourage continued practice by saying, "You get faster every time you practice" or comment, "It's nice you want to be a really fast runner. Running is good exercise."

➤ *Does your child try to cover a mistake or avoid embarrassment by saying something that isn't true?*

Young children have a tendency to conceal the truth about a mistake or an embarrassing situation. Help your child be truthful by avoiding questions that will tempt her to lie. If your child accidentally spills something, don't ask, "Did you spill this juice?" Instead try, "I see the juice is spilled. Please get a rag and wipe it up."

➤ *Does your child distort reality in order to get what she wants?*

During this egocentric period of a young child's life, she might tell untruths in accordance with her own desires. If you ask, "Is your room clean?" your child may tell you it is—especially if she wishes this were true so she can be in your favor. First, avoid trapping her in a lie by saying, "Let's go see how you're doing cleaning your room." Then help your child figure out how to finish the task. Teach her to ask for help if the job seems overwhelming.

➤ *Is your child testing you to see if she can trick or tease you?*

If so, your child may be looking for some power or control. As children strive for independence, they need many opportunities to do things their way. Consider if your child has opportunities to make choices and be independent. On the other hand, your child may try to trick you into doing something for her that she is capable of doing herself. Be good natured, yet let her know you are on to her tricks; say, "I think you are fooling me." Children enjoy being able to pull one over on their parent(s). This type of manipulation of the truth is generally not too serious at this age.

➤ *Is your child telling you something that isn't true in order to avoid punishment or an unpleasant activity?*

Many children lie because they are worried about how angry their parent(s) will be or to avoid being punished for their misdeeds. Teach your child that you can be trusted to handle misbehavior with relative calm, and that your responses will be fair. In this way she will not fear your responses and will learn to respect you. Children feel more guilt and lie less often to people they respect.

True or Untrue: A Game

Describe some things that are true and some that are untrue. Start with simple things the child can see and end with behaviors. After each statement, have the child(ren) decide if it is true or untrue. Here are a few examples to help get the game started:

My shoes are _____ (name the color). (True)
The grass is purple. (Untrue)

I am wearing _____ (name the color) pants. (True)
My hair is blue. (Untrue)

Our gerbil's name is _____. (True)
He sleeps in a bed. (Untrue).

We have two teachers in our room. (True)
_____ (name of a child who is present) is missing today. (Untrue)

What if I pick up my toys and say my room is clean? (True)
What if I don't pick up my toys and say my room is clean? (Untrue)

What if I brush my teeth and say I'm done? (True)
What if I don't brush my teeth and say that I did? (Untrue)

What if I break a toy and tell a grown-up I did it? (True)
What if I break a toy and say someone else broke it? (Untrue)

Adapted with the permission of Simon & Schuster, Inc. from *Teaching Your Children Values*, by Linda and Richard Eyre. Copyright ©1993 by R.M. Eyre & Assoc.

Let your child know you feel it is important to tell the truth. Be truthful yourself. Adults are often unaware of how many times they unintentionally model lying. Adults exaggerate experiences the child knows are not true and give excuses that are not true in order to avoid unpleasant invitations. For example, you may say you liked dinner when your child knows it was mediocre at best. Children who are very literal in their interpretations may view this as an example of lying.

Much of a young child's misbehavior is impulsive. When she denies it, she may be worrying that if she did this "bad thing" she will be viewed as "bad." Reassure her that everyone makes mistakes. If she continues to deny something, consider that she may be telling you the truth. Demonstrate that you trust her by believing her. When she does tell the truth, label it as the truth (so she ties the word to her experiences). Let her know you appreciate it. Thank her for her honesty. When you know she has done something, you might say, "I see you ripped the poster when you were angry." If she denies it, call the argument to an end by saying, "I don't want to argue about lying." Focus instead on what can be done to make it right. Perhaps she needs to do a job to help pay for the ruined poster or tape it back together.

Work with Your Provider

Work with your provider so your child will receive consistent messages about the importance of truthfulness. Discuss situations that are recurring and develop a Plan for Action.

When to Get Help

Children who break rules, get caught, and fear punishment are likely to lie more frequently. Be sure that you are teaching your child to behave appropriately by guiding behavior rather than harsh discipline. If your child lies each time she is in a stressful situation, talk with a parent educator or counselor who specializes in working with families of young children.

For Further Reading

Ekman, Paul. *Why Kids Lie*. New York: Charles Scribner's Sons, 1989.

Eyre, Linda, and Richard Eyre. *Teaching Your Children Values*. New York: Simon & Schuster, 1993.

Kitzinger, Sheila, and Celia Kitzinger. *Tough Questions*. Boston: The Harvard Common Press, 1991.

A Plan for Action

To develop your Plan for Action, choose a goal that best fits your situation. Then determine three or four actions providers and parent(s) will take. Choose additional actions specific to the early childhood setting and home. Mark your choices on this summary or write them on the planning form that follows.

Sample goals for a child who is telling tall tales and falsehoods:
- Recognizes truthful statements in a game-like situation.
- Recognizes fantasy in books and television
- Improves self-esteem.
- Asks for what she wants in acceptable ways.
- Add your ideas.

Sample actions parent(s) and provider can take:
- Model truthfulness.
- Emphasize the importance of telling the truth.
- Reinforce truthfulness.
- Believe this child unless you saw something to the contrary.
- Teach the difference between real and pretend.
- Teach the difference between telling the truth and a lie.
- Provide creative storytelling opportunities.
- Avoid power struggles about the accuracy of tall tales.
- Identify when this child is teasing.

- Guide misbehavior in a fair and consistent manner.
- Be accepting of behavioral mistakes.
- Problem solve with this child about ways to get what he wants without lying.
- Avoid questions that tempt this child to lie.
- When this child has made a behavioral mistake, focus on setting things right (in a way that is directly related).
- Add your ideas.

Sample actions provider can take:
- Offer plenty of child-directed activities.
- Add your ideas.

Sample actions parent(s) can take:
- Give age-appropriate choices.
- Encourage your child to perform age-appropriate tasks independently.
- Talk with a parent educator or counselor. Share pertinent information with your provider.
- Add your ideas.

Parent(s) and Provider Action Form

Date:_____

Our plan for _____

              (CHILD'S NAME)

Goal

Write a realistic goal for this child using one of the examples from this chapter or one of your own.

_____

_____

_____

_____

Actions parent(s) and provider will take

Choose from those in this chapter or use your own ideas.

1. _____
2. _____
3. _____
4. _____

Actions provider will take

Choose from those in this chapter or use your own ideas.

1. _____
2. _____

Actions parent(s) will take

Choose from those in this chapter or use your own ideas.

1. _____
2. _____

We will check in to discuss progress or modify our plan on_____

(set a day six weeks to three months from now).

Signed

_____

(provider)

_____

(parent)

CHAPTER 8

You Can't Make Me: Power Struggles

I have to be really careful about the way I phrase things when I talk to Jacob. If I tell him to do something and he doesn't want to do it, we really have a battle. I don't think I should give in after I ask him to do something.

What Is It?

One type of power struggle occurs when an adult asks a child to do something and the child refuses. Children need opportunities to do things for themselves and to make their own decisions. This helps them learn to develop inner control and leads to healthy independence. Sometimes in their attempts to be independent, children resist adult requests or become upset when they don't get what they want. Other times adults intrude on a child's activity or demand that a child comply without much consideration for the individual. These situations can result in power struggles that, once started, are hard to call to an end. Adults working with young children can do a lot to help children develop independence. At the same time, they can increase the chances that children will follow directions without a power struggle.

Observe and Problem Solve

Ask the following questions as you observe the child who does not comply with adult requests. Your observations may lead you to appropriate ways to work with this child.

➤ *Does this child resist adult requests without thinking?*

Toddlers and some young preschool-aged children say no automatically. For example, if you ask a child if he wants juice, he may answer no, then cry when you don't give him any. Understand that when this child says no he may not mean it. Make questions more concrete by showing the juice container while asking him his preference. Ask questions that cannot be answered with a yes or no. Say, "How much juice do you want?" Some children say no in imitation of those around them. Childproof your play area so this child can explore without hazard and without hearing no as often. Avoid modeling "No!" by substituting "Stop" when you must keep him from doing something. Find ways to say yes to this child. You might say, "Yes, when the toys are cleaned up" or "Yes, you may, after you're done." When you must deny a child's request, briefly explain your reasoning. Say something like, "I don't want you to run inside because you might fall and hurt yourself." Find ways to let this child be independent by deciding what to play and allowing him to do many things for himself.

➤ *Does this child know how to do what you're asking? Does he understand all the instructions?*

If children are unsure of themselves, they may not do as asked. They also may hesitate before complying or watch others for clues about how to behave. Make sure the child is capable of performing the task. Don't assume he knows. Demonstrate or tell a child how to do what you want. Keep directions simple. Use understandable terms. Give only one- or two-part directions. The child will not be able to comply if he has heard only a portion of what he has been

One evening at an Early Childhood Family Education class, it was almost time for snack when a terrible noise came from the direction of the tables. Omarr had overturned Jesse, chair and all. When the children's teacher investigated, Omarr simply stated he wanted that chair. (He always sat at that table, in that chair.) His teacher explained that someone else was sitting there. Then she pointed out the only other chair still available. Omarr refused the last chair stating, "But my mom said I could sit there." The teacher explained that if he did not sit down he would miss snack. Then she turned her attention to the other children and ignored his protests. Omarr stood throughout snack and did not join the group again until their next activity.

The next week, the teacher braced herself for another power struggle as snack time approached. To her surprise, Omarr walked straight to the spot he had so vehemently refused the week before, and sat down.

told, or if he remembers only the first or last part of lengthy instructions. Reduce competing noise. Talk directly to this child. Have him repeat back to you what you have asked. Repeating your directions helps to ensure he has heard and helps to commit it to memory. Many children walk away from a job that seems overwhelming instead of asking for help. Make sure it is acceptable to ask for help. Point out how everyone needs help at times. You sometimes need help carrying the snack tray and other children may need help with their coats.

➤ *Does this child refuse or delay doing as asked because he is involved in an activity?*

Children who are pulled away from an activity in which they are involved delay a chore or less desirable activity by arguing and complaining. Warn this child an activity is about to come to an end or when he must put his things away. Remove an activity that is competing for his attention. Promise to return it when he has done what you have asked. Keep the daily routine and schedule predictable so the child knows what is

expected. Be consistent about cleanup and chores. Help him start his work on jobs.

➤ *Does this child refuse when you ask him directly?*

Giving children a direction from across the room is not very effective. Move close to this child before beginning directions, use understandable terms, keep directions short, and state them once before helping the child to get started. If the child doesn't begin to do as asked, offer the choice, "Do you want to do it yourself or shall I help you?" Sometimes a child will want help, and it is better that he has told you with words than shown you with inappropriate behavior. Other times this choice spurs independence. Let this child know that he can go on to the next activity when he does what you have asked. For example, say, "When you finish hanging your coat, you can join the game" or "When you get your shoes on, I'll be able to tie them for you." Avoid power struggles in other situations by offering different types of choices. Ask, "Do you want to clean in the block area or the housekeeping?" or "You may sit in this spot or this one. You pick."

➤ *Does this child continue to argue even after you've set a limit?*

Some children have learned that if they argue long enough or effectively enough they will get what they want. Some use arguing as a delay tactic. Call an argument to an end. Say, "You're trying to get me to change my mind and I am not going to. You need to stop asking now." Ignore further protests.

If you responded to the child's request before thinking, however, you can change your mind. Let him know you have reconsidered. Say something like, "I have thought about it a little more and I've changed my mind." Give any other reasons you have.

This child may be arguing as a way to keep you involved with him. Be sure you have met his need for attention. Attend to him many times during the day when he is not arguing. Some children who push, push, push may be looking for boundaries. Set limits that are reasonable for this child and stick to them. Be sure to recognize and comment on times when this child does as he is told. Let him know how helpful this is.

▶ *Do power struggles with this child usually turn into a tantrum?*

Choose your fights to avoid unnecessary power struggles and tantrums. Insist that things go your way only when it is really important. For example, it probably isn't a big deal if this child gets a drink just a few minutes before snack. However, you may need to insist that he sit in a certain spot during a large group activity so he can better pay attention. Make sure you are not asking this child to do too much. Reduce your expectations for the time being and see if this helps decrease power struggles. This child may be more willing to follow your lead if he has had plenty of opportunity to make decisions and control his own activities. Consider scheduling choice time early in this child's day so he takes direction better, at another time. For information on how to respond to a tantrum that results from a power struggle, see chapter 9, "I'll Kick and Scream Until I Get My Way: Temper Tantrums."

Work with the Parent(s)

It is easy to say that the child has learned to argue because the parent(s) give in to him at home. This isn't always the case. Some children try to control those around them from very early ages. These children are challenging to providers and parents. Being consistent at home and the early childhood setting will help reduce power struggles to some extent. Part of working with this type of child may mean not engaging in unnecessary disputes.

In other cases, you may witness the parent giving in to the child. You can understand how easy this would be when a child struggles with you about most everything. Sympathize with the parent(s) while working with them as they learn more effective techniques. Give them the information for parent(s) and discuss a Plan for Action.

When to Get Help

Consult with others in the field about your work with this child. Ask a consultant to observe your interactions. This person may be able to give specific ways to implement these suggestions. Learning to work effectively with children who are noncompliant is an essential skill for early childhood educators.

Techniques for Avoiding Power Struggles

• Develop a positive relationship.

• Be firm, fair, and friendly.

• Keep a sense of humor.

• Give this child opportunities to be powerful and to make decisions.

• Offer choices.

• Keep schedules and routines predictable.

• Be consistent with expectations for cleanup and chores.

• Move close to the child before giving directions.

• State directions once, then help the child get started.

• Choose your fights. Insist on your way only when it is really important.

• Call arguments to an end.

• Ignore further protests. Detach yourself from the argument.

• Comment on times a child is being cooperative and following directions.

Refusing adult requests (when it is the only behavior of concern) is not one for which services are readily available. However, if this is one among a group of upsetting or disruptive behaviors (such as difficulty controlling anger, negative attention getting, aggression, or severe tantrums), it may be appropriate to suggest that the parent seek parent education or family counseling.

For Further Reading

Essa, Eva. *A Practical Guide to Solving Preschool Behavior Problems.* Albany, NY: Delmar Publishers, 1990.

McCarney, Stephen, and Angela Bauer. *The Parent's Guide.* Columbia, MO: Hawthorne Educational Services, 1989.

Wycoff, Jerry, and Barbara Unell. *Discipline Without Shouting or Spanking.* New York: Meadowbrook Press, 1984.

Jacob argues about everything. Sometimes I get so tired of the constant battle I just give up.

What Is It?

One type of power struggle occurs when an adult asks a child to do something and the child refuses. Children need opportunities to do things for themselves and to make their own decisions. This helps them learn to develop internal control and leads to healthy independence. Sometimes in their attempts to be independent, children resist adult requests or become upset when they don't get what they want. Other times adults intrude on a child's activity or demand that a child comply without much consideration for the individual. These situations can result in power struggles that, once started, are hard to call to an end. You can do a lot to help your child develop independence. At the same time, you can increase the chances that your child will follow directions without a power struggle.

Observe and Problem Solve

Ask the following questions as you observe your child when he isn't complying with your requests. Your observations may lead you to appropriate ways to work with your child on this issue.

➤ *Does your child resist your requests without thinking?*

Toddlers and some young preschool-aged children say no automatically. For example, if you ask a child if he wants juice, he may answer no, then cry when you don't give him any. Understand that in these situations when your child says no he may not mean it. Make questions more concrete by showing the juice container while asking him his preference. Ask questions that cannot be answered with a yes or no. Say, "How much juice do you want?" Some children say no in imitation of those around them. Childproof your play area so your child can explore without hazard and without hearing no as often. Avoid modeling "No!" by substituting "Stop" when you must keep him from doing something. Find ways to say yes to your child. You might say, "Yes, when the toys are cleaned up" or "Yes, you may, after you're done." When you must deny his request, briefly explain your reasoning. Say something like, "I don't want you to run in the house because you might fall and hurt yourself." Find ways to let your child be independent by deciding what to play and allowing him to do many things for himself.

➤ *Does your child know how to do what you are asking? Does he understand all the instructions?*

If children are unsure of themselves, they may not do as asked. They also may hesitate before complying. Make sure your child is capable of performing the task. Don't assume he knows. Demonstrate or tell him how to do what you want. Keep directions simple. Use understandable terms. Give only one- or two-part directions. Your child will not be able to comply if he has heard only a portion of what he has been told, or if he remembers only the first or last part of lengthy instructions. Reduce competing noise. Talk directly to your child. Have him repeat back to you what you have asked. Repeating directions helps to ensure he has heard and helps to commit it to memory. Many children walk away from a job that seems overwhelming instead of asking for help. Make sure it is acceptable to ask for help. Point out how everyone needs help at times. You need help cleaning the house and Grandma needs help carrying groceries.

➤ *Does your child refuse or delay doing as asked because he is involved in an activity?*

Children who are pulled away from an activity in which they are involved delay a chore or less desirable activity by arguing and complaining. Warn your child an activity is about to come to an end or when he must put his things away. Remove any activity that is competing for his attention. Promise to return it when he has done what you have asked. Keep your daily routine and schedule predictable so your child knows what is expected. Be consistent about cleanup and chores. Help him start his work on jobs.

➤ *Does your child refuse when you ask him directly?*

Giving your child a direction from across the room is not very effective. Move close to your child before beginning directions, use understandable terms, keep directions short, and state them once before helping him to get started. If your child doesn't begin to do as asked, offer the choice, "Do you want to do it yourself or shall I help you?" Sometimes a child will want help, and it is better that he has told you with words than shown you with inappropriate behavior. Other times this choice spurs independence. Let your child know that he can go on to the next activity, when he does as you have asked. For example, say, "When you hang up your coat we will be able to play a game" or "When you get your shoes on I'll be able to tie them for you." Avoid power struggles in other situations by offering different types of choices. Ask, "Do you want to wear the blue shirt or the green one?" or "Do you want to come now or in two minutes?"

➤ *Does your child continue to argue even after you've set a limit?*

When an adult gives in, children learn that if they argue long enough or effectively enough they will get what they want. There are a number of reasons parents give in to their child's requests. They may be distracted by other things, feel guilty about leaving their child in an early childhood program, think it is easier, or change their mind. Make your decisions about what your child is asking based on what is best for your child in the long run—not what is easier at the moment. Call any argument to an end. Say, "You are trying to get me to change my mind and I am not going to. You need to stop asking now." Ignore further protests.

If you responded to the child's request before thinking, however, you can change your mind. Let him know you have reconsidered. Say something like, "I have thought about it a little more and I've changed my mind." Give any other reasons you have.

This child may be arguing as a way to keep you involved with him. Be sure you have met his need for attention. Attend to him many times each day when he is not arguing. Some children who push, push, push may be looking for boundaries. Set limits that are reasonable for your child and stick to them. Be sure to recognize and comment on times when your child does as he is told. Let him know how helpful this is.

➤ *Do power struggles with your child usually turn into a tantrum?*

Choose your fights to avoid unnecessary power struggles and tantrums. Insist that things go your way only when it is really important. For example, it probably isn't a big deal if your child wants to wear the new pajamas you bought him even though they are too big. However, you may need to insist that he eats a nutritious snack rather than junk food. Make sure you are not asking your child to do too much. Reduce your expectations for the time being and see if this helps decrease power struggles. Consider allowing enough time after returning from your early childhood program to play before requiring him to follow directions. When he has had self-directed time first, he may follow your directions at another time more willingly. For information on how to respond to a tantrum that results from a power struggle, see chapter 9, "I'll Kick and Scream Until I Get My Way: Temper Tantrums."

Work with Your Provider

Children who like to control can seem oppositional at times. These children are challenging to work with. Being consistent at home and in the early childhood setting will help reduce power struggles to some extent. Part of learning to live with your child may mean not engaging in unnecessary disputes. Work with your provider to develop a Plan for Action.

When to Get Help

Refusing adult requests (when it is the only behavior of concern) is not one for which services are readily available. However, if this is one among a group of upsetting or disruptive behaviors (such as difficulty controlling anger, negative attention getting, aggression, or severe tantrums), it may be appropriate to seek education or family counseling to help your child learn more acceptable behaviors.

For Further Reading

McCarney, Stephen, and Angela Bauer. *The Parent's Guide*. Columbia, MO: Hawthorne Educational Services, 1989.
Wycoff, Jerry, and Barbara Unell. *Discipline Without Shouting or Spanking*. New York: Meadowbrook Press, 1984.

A Plan for Action

To develop your Plan for Action, choose a goal that best fits your situation. Then determine three or four actions providers and parent(s) will take. Choose additional actions specific to the early childhood setting and home. Mark your choices on this summary or write them on the planning form that follows.

Sample goals for a child who engages in power struggles:
- Stops and thinks before answering questions.
- Follows _____-part directions.
- Follows directions the first time he is asked.
- Follows directions without arguing.
- Add your ideas.

Sample actions parent(s) and providers can take:
- Keep schedules and routines predictable.
- Warn this child of a change in activities.
- Keep expectations consistent during cleanup and chores.
- Allow this child to do many things for himself.
- Ask questions that can't be answered with a yes or no.
- Make questions/choices concrete.
- Move close to this child before giving directions.
- Use understandable terms when giving directions.
- Give only one- or two-part directions.
- Have this child repeat directions.
- State directions once, then move to help.
- Comment on times this child follows directions.
- Teach this child the task he is being asked to perform.
- Help this child get started with jobs.

- Make it clear the assigned task needs to be done before this child starts the next activity.
- Find ways to say yes to this child.
- Think before responding to this child's requests.
- Choose your fights. Insist only when it is really important.
- When saying no to this child, briefly explain your reasoning.
- Call arguments to an end.
- Ignore protests.
- Add your ideas.

Sample actions provider can take:
- Schedule time for this child to be self-directed when he arrives.
- Have a consultant observe your interactions. Share pertinent information with the parent(s).
- Add your ideas.

Sample actions parent(s) can take:
- Make decisions based on what is best for this child in the long run.
- Talk with a parent educator or counselor. Share pertinent information with your provider.
- Add your ideas.

Parent(s) and Provider Action Form

Date:_____

Our plan for _____
             (CHILD'S NAME)

Goal

Write a realistic goal for this child using one of the examples from this chapter or one of your own.

_____

_____

_____

_____

Actions parent(s) and provider will take

Choose from those in this chapter or use your own ideas.

1. _____
2. _____
3. _____
4. _____

Actions provider will take

Choose from those in this chapter or use your own ideas.

1. _____
2. _____

Actions parent(s) will take

Choose from those in this chapter or use your own ideas.

1. _____
2. _____

We will check in to discuss progress or modify our plan on_____

(set a day six weeks to three months from now).

Signed

_____

(provider)

_____

(parent)

CHAPTER 9

I'll Kick and Scream Until I Get My Way: Temper Tantrums

Angelique threw a huge tantrum when I took away the paper she was holding. She had picked up Andrea's by mistake and was convinced it was her own. When I gave her the right one, she started screaming. She ripped up the paper, threw it on the floor, and stomped on it. I gave her paper to make another one at home but she kept on screaming.

What Is It?

Children as young as two years old may have temper tantrums when they do not get what they want or when they become extremely frustrated. They may also have temper tantrums when someone asks them to do something they don't want to do. This emotional outburst is easily recognized when a child kicks, cries or screams, throws things, bangs about, or throws herself to the floor. An older child may replace the physical demonstration of emotion with loud, angry verbal protests.

Tantrums reach different levels of intensity depending upon whether or not children receive attention, believe they will get what they want, and learn more effective coping skills. Young children may not have the language needed to express how they feel and can become anxious about these overwhelming feelings. Children of all ages can get locked into a tantrum and not know how to stop the rush of emotions. You can help children learn to express themselves in

more satisfactory ways as well as support them when they do lose control.

Observe and Problem Solve

To better understand how to help a child who has tantrums, observe what leads up to the outburst. Watch the child in a variety of situations. Use the suggestions that follow as you decide on the most appropriate course of action.

➤ *Does this child tantrum because she is frustrated by a task?*

Some children become frustrated when they try to do a task they are not yet skilled enough to perform. Provide many activities with varying skill levels from which children may choose. Steer children to choices that best match their abilities. Teach them to avoid, for the time being, those that are too hard. Say, "Let's look for a puzzle with about six pieces." Intervene as this child is becoming frustrated. Help her learn to recognize her own tolerance level. Say, "It looks like you're getting frustrated. Take a break, count to ten, or take a few big breaths." Encourage this child to ask for help. Point out how you need help cleaning the room and someone else needs help tying their shoe. Teach her safe ways to express herself when she is angry. She can stamp her feet, yell, crumple paper, tell someone, or pound playdough. When this child is being patient, comment on it.

➤ *Does this child see others tantrum and imitate their behavior?*

Many young children imitate the behavior of those around them. Pay attention to this child many times a day when she is behaving appropriately. When she watches someone else who is

80

having a tantrum, let her know the other child is having a hard time. Get her interested in some other activity. Praise her for having ideas of her own.

Be careful not to model emotional outbursts yourself. Recognize your own need to take a break. Use words to name your feelings. Demonstrate how to calm down by listening to music, looking at a book, singing, drawing, or playing. Avoid demanding that things are done *now*. This child may think she has the right to demand what she wants *now* too.

➤ *Does this child tantrum more frequently when she is tired, sick, or hungry?*

Most people find it difficult to cope when they are tired, sick, or hungry. Children are even more prone to outbursts under these circumstances. Meeting this child's basic needs will help to reduce the risk of tantrums. Vary your schedule to accommodate this child and others who may be over tired or hungry. Avoid new or challenging activities during times of the day this child is fatigued. Late afternoon and just before nap or lunch are particularly taxing times for children. Understand that emotions are close to the surface the day before a child is ill. If possible, anticipate other situations that may cause this child to tantrum. Common triggers include: playing with other children when this child needs alone time, being asked to perform a chore that appears overwhelming, having too many changes in activity, or having too much going on at one time.

➤ *Does this child tantrum when you set a limit?*

Asking this child to join a group activity or pick up toys when she doesn't want to may cause an outburst. Arrange your environment so that this child routinely helps herself to appropriate materials and helps to put them away. Place coat hooks at eye level, arrange materials so she can choose from what is available, and clearly mark where things go so she can put them away independently. Provide choices when possible. When you must set a limit, be firm. Remember not to take outbursts personally. Do not let her outbursts sway you. For more help coping with outbursts, see chapter 8, "You Can't Make Me: Power Struggles."

➤ *Does this child tantrum when she is denied an activity or an object she wants?*

Some children believe they will get what they want through their outbursts. When you deny this child something, for good reason, do not give in. Detach yourself from the situation by focusing on something else or walking away. Don't try to explain or talk with this child while she is upset. Ignore the outburst. Listen for a break in crying and watch for signals she is calming down. Move close to this child to offer comfort and support. When the tantrum is over, do not lecture. Help this child become engaged in an activity. If she brings up the difficult situation, problem solve how to handle it the next time it happens. Resist the temptation to ask this child, "Why did you get so upset?" Very few children have the verbal skills or sufficient understanding of their own behavior to explain it.

➤ *Is this child destructive or hurtful during a tantrum?*

When a child is destructive or hurtful, you may need to respond in ways that will protect people and property. Make sure you remain calm when dealing with a child who tantrums. Help all the other children move away. If another child is hurt, attend to her (instead of the one who is having a tantrum). Tell the hurt child you are sorry it happened. Do not use the other child's name or blame them in any way. Stay near the child who is having a tantrum. Be aware of what she is doing while pretending to attend to something else. Once the tantrum stops, go to this child and sit near her without talking. When this child is ready, help her clean anything disrupted during the outburst. Then get her started in an activity. Some children want to be physically held once they have calmed down. Others fight it. Respect her choice.

➤ *Does this child seem locked into the tantrum or unable to stop?*

Some outbursts begin as an attempt to get what is wanted, others begin as the last straw in a frustrating or overwhelming day. However they begin, a child can become locked in. This child will need your help to stop. Prevent situations that lead to tantrums. If she gets stuck in tantrums frequently, you may need to intervene differently than previously recommended. Move to this child. Let her know you understand she is upset. Distract her to another activity. If she does get locked in and the tantrum lasts more than ten to fifteen minutes, tell her, "It's time to stop now." Help her take deep, relaxing breaths. Get more information about how to help a child who tantrums by taking a class or reading more about it.

Work with the Parent(s)

Many parents work with their children to teach them appropriate ways to get their needs met. A few, however, give in to the child's demands and reinforce tantruming. You will not be able to control all the factors that keep temper tantrums going. Do what you can in your setting to be consistent and firm. Give the parent(s) the information that follows. Use the Plan for Action to discuss what you can do to work together. Consistency between home and the early childhood setting will give this child a clear message that there are times she cannot have her way.

When to Get Help

Suggest the child's parent(s) contact a parent educator or family counselor who specializes in working with young children if this child tantrums each time she is in a stressful situation or is denied her way; if the child's tantrums seem filled with extreme anger; or if you do not see a significant decrease in tantrums despite your efforts.

For Further Reading

Kurcinka, Mary Sheedy. *Raising Your Spirited Child*. New York: Harper Perennial, 1991.

McCarney, Stephen, and Angela Bauer. *The Parent's Guide*. Columbia, MO: Hawthorne Educational Services, 1989.

Rubin, Douglas. *Bratbusters*. El Paso, TX: Skidmore-Roth Publishing, 1992.

Angelique lay on the floor of the store and kicked and screamed for ten minutes. I was so embarrassed. All that carrying on because I got the wrong cereal. I was already in line and I wasn't going back just for that.

What Is It?

Children as young as two years old may have temper tantrums when they do not get what they want or when they become extremely frustrated. They may also have temper tantrums when someone asks them to do something they don't want to do. This emotional outburst is easily recognized when a child kicks, cries or screams, throws things, bangs about, or throws herself to the floor. An older child may replace the physical demonstration of emotion with loud, angry verbal protests.

Tantrums reach different levels of intensity depending upon whether or not children receive attention, believe they will get what they want, and learn more effective coping skills. Young children may not have the language needed to express how they feel and can become anxious about these overwhelming feelings. Children of all ages can get locked into a tantrum and not know how to stop the rush of emotions. You can help your child learn to express herself in more satisfactory ways as well as support her when she does lose control.

Observe and Problem Solve

To better understand how to help your child, observe what leads up to outbursts. Watch your child in a variety of situations. Use the suggestions that follow as you decide on the most appropriate course of action.

➤ *Does your child tantrum because she is frustrated by a task?*

Some children become frustrated when they try to do a task they are not yet skilled enough to perform. Provide activities that are easy enough for your child to do. Teach her to avoid, for the time being, those that are too hard. Say, "Let's look for your puzzle instead of this hard one." Step in as she becomes frustrated. Help her learn to recognize her own tolerance level. Say, "It looks like you're getting frustrated. Take a break, count to ten, or take a few big breaths." Encourage your child to ask for help. Point out how you need help cleaning the house and her brother needs help tying his shoes. Teach her safe ways to express herself when she is angry. She can stamp her feet, yell, crumple paper, tell someone, or pound playdough. When your child is being patient, comment on it.

➤ *Does your child see others tantrum and imitate their behavior?*

Many young children imitate the behavior of those around them. Pay attention to your child many times a day when she is behaving appropriately. When she watches someone else who is having a tantrum, let her know the other child is having a hard time. Get her interested in some other activity. Praise her for having ideas of her own.

Be careful not to model emotional outbursts yourself. Recognize your own need to take a break. Use words to name your feelings. Demonstrate how to calm down by listening to music, looking at a book, singing, drawing, or playing. Avoid demanding that things are done *now*. Your child may think she has the right to demand what she wants *now* too.

➤ *Does your child tantrum more frequently when she is tired, sick, or hungry?*

Most people find it difficult to cope when they are tired, sick, or hungry. Children are even more prone to outbursts under these circumstances. Meeting this child's basic needs will help to reduce the risk of tantrums. Vary your schedule to meet the needs of your child when she is over tired or hungry. Avoid stressful situations like shopping or visiting friends during times of the day when your child is fatigued. Late afternoon and just before nap or lunch are particularly taxing times for children. Understand that emotions are close to the surface the day before your child is ill. If possible, anticipate other situations that may cause your child to tantrum. Common triggers include: playing with other children when she needs alone time, being asked to perform a chore that appears overwhelming, having too many changes in routine, or having too much going on at one time.

➤ *Does your child tantrum when you set a limit?*

Asking your child to do something for you or to pick up toys when she doesn't want to may cause an outburst. Arrange your environment so that your child routinely helps herself to appropriate materials and helps to put them away. Place coat hooks at eye level, arrange materials so she can choose from what is available, and clearly mark where things go so she can put them away. Provide choices whenever possible. When you must set a limit, be firm. Remember not to take outbursts personally. Do not let her outbursts sway you. For more help coping with outbursts, see chapter 8, "You Can't Make Me: Power Struggles."

➤ *Does your child tantrum when she is denied an activity or an object she wants?*

Some children believe they will get what they want through their outbursts. When you deny your child something, for good reason, do not give in. Detach yourself from the situation by focusing on something else or walking away. Don't try to explain or talk with your child while she is upset. Ignore the outburst. Listen for a break in crying and watch for signals she is calming down. Move close to her to offer comfort and support. When the tantrum is over, do not lecture. Help your child become engaged in an activity. If she brings up the difficult situation, problem solve how to handle it the next time it happens. Resist the temptation to ask your child, "Why did you get so upset?" Very few children have the verbal skills or sufficient understanding of their own behavior to explain it.

➤ *Is your child destructive or hurtful during a tantrum?*

When a child is destructive or hurtful, you may need to respond in ways that will protect people and property. Remain calm yourself. Move away from your child but not too far. Be aware of what she is doing while pretending to attend to something else. Once the tantrum stops, go to your child and sit near her without talking. When your child is ready, help her clean anything disrupted during the outburst. Then help her get started in an activity. Some children want to be physically held once they have calmed down. Others fight it. Respect her choice.

➤ *Does your child seem locked into the tantrum or unable to stop?*

Some outbursts begin as an attempt to get what is wanted, others begin as the last straw in a frustrating or overwhelming day. However they begin, your child can become locked in. She will need your help to stop. Prevent situations that lead to tantrums. If she gets stuck in tantrums frequently, you may need to intervene in different ways than previously recommended. Move to this child. Let her know you understand she is upset. Distract her to another activity. If she does get locked in and the tantrum lasts more than ten to fifteen minutes, tell her, "It's time to stop now." Help her take deep, relaxing breaths.

Work with Your Provider
Be consistent and firm when you set limits. Meet with your provider to discuss how you will work together. Consistency between home and the early childhood setting will give your child a clear message that there are times she cannot have her way.

When to Get Help
Contact a parent educator or counselor who specializes in working with young children if your child tantrums each time she is in a stressful situation or is denied her way; if your child's tantrums seem filled with extreme anger; or if you do not see a significant decrease in tantrums despite your efforts.

For Further Reading
Kurcinka, Mary Sheedy. *Raising Your Spirited Child.* New York: Harper Perennial, 1991.

McCarney, Stephen, and Angela Bauer. *The Parent's Guide.* Columbia, MO: Hawthorne Educational Services, 1989.

Rubin, Douglas. *Bratbusters.* El Paso, TX: Skidmore-Roth Publishing, 1992.

A Plan for Action

To develop your Plan for Action, choose a goal that best fits your situation. Then determine three or four actions providers and parent(s) will take. Choose additional actions specific to the early childhood setting and home. Mark your choices on this summary or write them on the planning form that follows.

Sample goals for a child who has temper tantrums:
- Increases frustration tolerance.
- Follows directions the first time asked.
- Uses words to express frustration or anger.
- Add your ideas.

Sample actions parent(s) and provider can take:
- Offer developmentally appropriate activities for this child.
- Intervene when this child is becoming frustrated.
- Encourage this child to ask for help.
- Teach this child safe ways to express anger.
- Model words to use as you express your own emotions.
- Avoid challenging or new activities at times of the day this child is tired.
- When this child is being patient, comment on it.
- Be firm, fair, and friendly when setting limits.
- State the limit and the reason why only one time. Then do not argue.
- When limits are set for good reason, remain firm even if she tantrums.
- Ignore emotional outbursts.
- Remain calm by detaching yourself from the situation.
- When there is an outburst, listen for a break in crying.
- Move close to this child after an outburst; offer comfort and support.
- Help this child take deep relaxing breaths.
- After the outburst, help this child clean up anything that was disrupted.
- When she is calm, help this child become engaged in an activity.
- If the tantrum lasts more than ten to fifteen minutes, tell this child it is time to stop.
- Add your ideas.

Sample actions provider can take:
- Help other children move away from a child who is having a tantrum so they do not get injured.
- Learn more about how to help this child. Share pertinent information with the parent(s).
- Add your ideas.

Sample actions parent(s) can take:
- Talk with a parent educator or counselor. Share pertinent information with your provider.
- Add your ideas.

Parent(s) and Provider Action Form

Date:_____

Our plan for _____
                    (CHILD'S NAME)

Goal

Write a realistic goal for this child using one of the examples from this chapter or one of your own.

_____

_____

_____

_____

Actions parent(s) and provider will take

Choose from those in this chapter or use your own ideas.

1. _____
2. _____
3. _____
4. _____

Actions provider will take

Choose from those in this chapter or use your own ideas.

1. _____
2. _____

Actions parent(s) will take

Choose from those in this chapter or use your own ideas.

1. _____
2. _____

We will check in to discuss progress or modify our plan on_____
(set a day six weeks to three months from now).

Signed

_____
(provider)

_____
(parent)

CHAPTER 10

Let's Say I'm Batman: Superhero Play

I have a few children in my group who only want to play superheroes. Just about every day I hear Ernie say, "I'm Batman, you be Robin, and Joey is Joker. Let's say we go after him in our Batmobile."

What Is It?

Many girls and boys are drawn to the fast action and exciting themes of superhero play. As in other types of play, they learn how to cooperate, sequence a story, negotiate how play will continue, as well as use important language skills. In this type of dramatic play, children work on their understandings of good and evil, power and control, right and wrong, and real and pretend. Adults sometimes find this play difficult to supervise because it has a tendency to become loud and aggressive. It also may include violent themes. But when providers look closely at the play and become involved in it, they can help to keep a lid on this exciting play and expand the learning taking place.

Observe and Problem Solve

Keep the following questions in mind when watching the children who are most likely to be involved in this type of play. Then use the suggestions to effectively guide superhero play while allowing children to work through their understanding of these themes.

➤ *What are the popular themes of play?*

Many of the themes are likely to be related to television programs or movies. Watch the pro-grams that influence their play. When you know the story lines and what the characters are likely to do, you will be able to give viable suggestions that expand the play. For instance, on one of the Power Ranger episodes, Zach helps out at a camp. Use this information to suggest that the children pretend to go canoeing or horseback riding as they might at camp.

Find ways to introduce children to other exciting play themes that are not related to a television program. Read books and visit a zoo or museum. Pack a bag and take an imaginary trip to the land of the dinosaurs; go on a photo safari; explore cardboard box "caves" with a flashlight and magnifying glass; cross a river of hot lava on rope spread on the floor; or build a spaceship to escape the slime monster from Mars.

➤ *What are the underlying issues the child may be trying to understand?*

Preschool children struggle with their feelings about control and power. By pretending to be a superhero, a child has a chance to feel powerful. Look for ways the child can be powerful in your setting. He can help to make rules, decide what book to read or where to play, or show you his strong muscles as he climbs to the top of the playground equipment. Another child may use this type of play to conquer fears. You can help that child learn to get rid of the monsters by ordering them out of here "Right now!" For another, the line between what is real and what is pretend may not be very clear. Identify these feelings by asking, "Some things seem very real, don't they?" Discuss how actors are so good at pretending that it looks real. Act out favorite stories (such as Three Billy Goats

Gruff) so this child has an opportunity to be the actor.

➤ *Does the child create new story lines or merely imitate things he has seen?*

In dramatic play, children often start with things they have seen or experienced and then create stories that go beyond their experiences. If a child seems stuck and merely imitates what he has seen, join the play as one of the characters. Expand on his idea by making suggestions that are closely related to his current play. Be careful not to move the story too far from what he is playing or he may reject your suggestions. For example, if he is playing that Spiderman is fighting crime and you suggest he take Spiderman to a movie he probably won't see any connection and will not go along with your idea. If one suggestion doesn't work, try another. Help him move his own story along by commenting on what you observe and asking open-ended questions. Say, "The Ninja Turtles are using their powers on Shredder again. What will they do next?" If needed, suggest that the turtles are hungry. Maybe he could make a pepperoni pizza for them.

➤ *Does the child use toys and props that allow creativity?*

Some of the toys that are marketed for superhero play are made to look as if they are to be used in only one way. The advertising makes a child believe that he needs more toys to perform other functions. (For example, supposedly Bath Time Barbie is the only Barbie doll that can go in the tub. If you want a doll to exercise, marketers want you to believe you must buy another for that purpose.) When choosing toys, look for those that allow the child to use them in

a number of ways (such as Lego or Lincoln Log building blocks). Have the child create his own props to support play. After suggesting the Ninja Turtles were hungry, get out scissors and construction paper or playdough and let the child make a pizza.

➤ *Does this child include weapons as part of his superhero play?*

Many people have strong feelings about allowing children to pretend to use weapons in early childhood settings. Yet it seems no matter what providers say, someone fashions a weapon even if it is made out of toast! Redirect the child by reminding him to eat his toast and showing him more productive props. Encourage children to develop incredible items (like Inspector Gadget might have) to aid in tracking the danger. Can they make a radar detector, walkie-talkie, or a trap? Get them to work to protect the town against a natural disaster such as a forest fire, hurricane, or a gorilla that has escaped from the zoo. These suggestions take the focus off fighting other people and on to a cooperative effort.

➤ *What are the signals this play is getting out of control?*

Tune into the individual's signals that play is getting too chaotic or that he needs help to resolve a problem. Watch for more aggression; a louder, higher pitched voice; more arguments about who will do what; and trouble sharing props. Although adults are quick to stop the play or redirect it at this point, what the child probably needs is help learning to accept changes in play and solve problems. Practice conflict resolution. Identify the problem. Think of ways it could be worked out. Decide on the best solution. Then try it out. If it doesn't work, try another.

If you must draw this type of play to a close, do so with a logical ending to the story. Say, "After a big pizza supper, the Ninja Turtle is very sleepy; put him to bed for a while and choose something quiet to do." Have water, sand, shaving cream, or playdough available as calming activities. Have children who have been playing together for some time take a break from this type of cooperative play and play side by side or alone.

➤ *What does the child need to learn about peacemaking?*

Balance the violence children see and learn by teaching cooperation and peacemaking. During superhero play say, "It seems like the Power Rangers only know how to solve problems by fighting. What else could they do?" De-emphasize competition by playing cooperative games and planning cooperative learning activities.

Work with the Parent(s)

Talk with the parent(s) about limiting the amount of violent programming to which their child is exposed. It is unlikely that families who view these programs will eliminate this type of television so suggest that they watch one fewer program. Describe some of the different themes the child has enjoyed in your setting that still allow him to be powerful. Include some of the creative scenarios that the child has developed. They may be able to extend this type of play at home. Use the Plan for Action to discuss how to proceed in working with this child.

When to Get Help

If play remains repetitive over a number of months despite your continued efforts to expand it, talk with an early childhood consultant about ways to work with this child. If play is excessively gruesome or violent, consider referring the family to a parent educator or counselor who specializes in working with young children.

Effective Ways to Respond to Superhero Play

- Suggest a new scene related to the story.
- Search for or make a new prop.
- Join the play yourself.
- Weave a rest time into the play by describing a quiet activity their characters are likely to engage in.
- Put limits on the use of weapons.
- Draw play to a close with a logical end to the story or smooth transition to the next activity.

For Further Reading

Carlsson-Paige, Nancy, and Diane Levin. *Who's Calling the Shots?* Philadelphia: New Society Publishing, 1990.

Crary, Elizabeth. *Kids Can Cooperate.* Seattle: Parenting Press, 1984.

Fry-Miller, Kathleen, and Judith Myers-Wells. *Young Peacemakers Project Book.* Elgin, IL: Brethren Press, 1988.

Park, Mary Joan. *Peacemaking for Little Friends.* St. Paul: Little Friends for Peace, 1985.

Sobel, Jeffrey. *Everybody Wins: 393 Non-Competitive Games for Young Children.* New York: Walker and Company, 1983.

One day I overheard my son say to his younger brother, "Want to fight? I'm Batman and you be Mr. Rogers! I've got a mega blaster for my weapon."

What Is It?

Many girls and boys are drawn to the fast action and exciting themes of superhero play. As in other types of play, they learn how to cooperate, sequence a story, negotiate how play will continue, as well as use important language skills. In this type of dramatic play, children work on their understandings of good and evil, power and control, right and wrong, and real and pretend. Parents are sometimes concerned about this type of play because it has a tendency to become loud and aggressive. It may also include violent themes. When you become involved in the play, you can help to keep a lid on it, influence your child's understanding of many important themes, and expand the learning taking place.

Observe and Problem Solve

Keep the following questions in mind when watching your child as he engages in this type of play. Then use the suggestions to effectively guide superhero play while still allowing him to work through his understanding of themes expressed.

➤ *What are the popular themes of play?*

Many of the themes are likely to be related to television programs or movies. You may want to limit the number of programs your child watches if he seems unable or unwilling to engage in dramatic play that reflects other experiences he has had. Watch with him whatever programming you do allow so that you will know the characters and story line. Use what you know about the program to provide viable suggestions that expand the play. For instance, on one of the Power Ranger episodes, Zach helps out at a camp. Use this information to suggest

that your child pretend to go canoeing or horseback riding as he might at camp.

Find ways to introduce your child to other exciting play themes that are not related to a television program. Read books and visit a zoo or museum. Pack a bag and take an imaginary trip to the land of the dinosaurs; go on a photo safari; explore cardboard box "caves" with a flashlight and magnifying glass; cross a river of hot lava on rope spread on the floor; or build a spaceship to escape the slime monster from Mars.

➤ *What are the underlying issues your child may be trying to understand?*

Preschool children struggle with their feelings about control and power. By pretending to be a superhero, your child has a chance to feel powerful. Look for ways your child can be powerful at home. He can help to make rules, decide to have spaghetti or pizza for supper, or show you his strong muscles as he helps to rearrange the furniture. If your child seems to be using this type of play to conquer fears, help him learn to get rid of monsters by ordering them out of here "Right now!" If your child is having difficulty determining the line between what is real and what is pretend, identify his feelings by asking, "Some things seem very real, don't they?" Discuss how actors are so good at pretending that it looks real. Act out some favorite stories (such as Three Billy Goats Gruff) so he has an opportunity to be the actor.

➤ *Does your child create new story lines or merely imitate things he has seen?*

In dramatic play, children often start with things they have seen or experienced and then create stories that go beyond their experiences. If your child seems stuck and merely imitates what he has seen, help him by becoming one of the characters. Comment on what you observe and ask open-ended questions to help move him along. Say, "The Ninja Turtles are using their powers on Shredder again. What will they do next?" If needed, expand his play by making a suggestion that is closely related to his current theme. Be careful not to move too far from what he is playing or he may reject your suggestions.

Suggest that the turtles are hungry and make a pepperoni pizza for them. Be creative. If one suggestion doesn't work, try another related story line.

➤ *Does your child use toys and props that allow creativity?*

Some of the toys that are marketed for super-hero play are made to look as if they are to be used in only one way. The advertising makes a child believe that he needs more toys to perform other functions. (For example, supposedly Bath Time Barbie is the only Barbie doll that can go in the tub. If you want a doll to exercise, mar-keters want you to believe you must buy an-other for that purpose.) When choosing toys, look for those that allow your child to use them in a number of ways (such as Lego or Lincoln Log building blocks). Have your child create his own props to support play. After suggesting the Ninja Turtles were hungry, get out scissors and construction paper or playdough and let your child make a pizza.

➤ *Does your child include weapons as part of his super-hero play?*

Many people have strong feelings about allow-ing young children to pretend to use weapons. Direct his play to more productive props. En-courage your child to develop incredible items (like Inspector Gadget might have) to aid in tracking the danger. Can he make a radar detec-tor, walkie-talkie, or a trap? Have your child work to protect your family from a natural dis-aster such as a forest fire, hurricane, or a gorilla that has escaped from the zoo. These sugges-tions take the focus off fighting other people.

➤ *What are the signals this play is getting out of con-trol?*

Tune into your child's signals that play is getting too chaotic or that he needs help to resolve a problem. Watch for more aggression; a louder, higher pitched voice; throwing of toys; and more arguments. Although adults are quick to stop the play or redirect it at this point, what your child probably needs is help learning to accept changes in play and solve problems. Practice problem solving. Identify the problem. ("I'm trying to work and your play is getting too

noisy.") Think of ways it could be worked out. ("How could we work it out so we both get what we want?") Decide on the best solution. ("Let's try your idea to move your things into your bed-room, but then if it continues to be too loud, you will have to think of something quiet to do.") Try it out. If it doesn't work, follow through on the consequence you made.

If you must draw this type of play to a close, do so with a logical ending to the story. Say, "After a big pizza supper, the Ninja Turtle is very sleepy; put him to bed for a while and choose something quiet to do." Have books, crayons, puzzles, or playdough available as calming activities.

➤ *What does your child need to learn about peacemaking?*

Balance the violence your child sees and learns by teaching cooperation and peacemaking. Dur-ing superhero play say, "It seems like the Power Rangers only know how to solve problems by fighting. What else could they do?" Do things around the house cooperatively, such as work to-gether to make a fruit salad or wash the car. Read a book in which there is a conflict. Stop the story before the end and let your child figure out a peaceful ending. Play house, doctor, or veteri-narian where you practice caring for others.

Work with Your Provider

Superhero play is much easier to guide and allow at home than it usually is in a group set-ting. The large number of children in a group setting makes it difficult to cope with the noise and activity level that typically accompanies this type of play. Aggressiveness during superhero play adds additional difficulties for providers. Your provider may ask you to help in putting su-perhero play into perspective by limiting the amount of time spent in this play and the amount of violent television or movies your child views. It can be difficult to control all media ex-posure to violence. However, try to carefully choose the programming your preschool-aged child routinely watches.

When to Get Help

If play remains repetitive over a number of months despite your continued efforts to expand it, or if play is excessively gruesome or violent, consider talking with a parent educator or counselor who specializes in working with children.

For Further Reading

Carlsson-Paige, Nancy, and Diane Levin. *Who's Calling the Shots?* Philadelphia: New Society Publishing, 1990.

Crary, Elizabeth. *Kids Can Cooperate*. Seattle: Parenting Press, 1984.

Fry-Miller, Kathleen, and Judith Myers-Wells. *Young Peacemakers Project Book*. Elgin, IL: Brethren Press, 1988.

Park, Mary Joan. *Peacemaking for Little Friends*. St. Paul: Little Friends for Peace, 1985.

A Plan for Action

To develop your Plan for Action, choose a goal that best fits your situation. Then determine three or four actions providers and parent(s) will take. Choose additional actions specific to the early childhood setting and home. Mark your choices on this summary or write them on the planning form that follows.

Sample goals for a child who plays superhero themes excessively:
- Plays themes other than superheroes.
- Expands play beyond imitation of television shows.
- Creates his own props.
- Engages in quiet activity when superhero play is drawn to a close.
- Takes part in peacemaking or cooperative activities.
- Add your ideas.

Sample actions parent(s) and provider can take:
- Offer open-ended toys and materials.
- Have calming activities available.
- Recognize times this child is being strong outside of superhero play.
- Allow this child to help set rules and make choices.
- Become familiar with television shows influencing play.
- Identify feelings that are enacted during superhero play.
- Join the play and help direct it.
- Make suggestions that expand this child's play.
- Provide materials so this child can make his own props.
- Step in and redirect play before it escalates out of control.
- Provide a logical end to the story when this play must end.
- Practice problem solving when needed.
- Introduce play themes that are not related to television.
- Teach about peacemaking and cooperation.
- Add your ideas.

Sample actions provider can take:
- Have children play side by side for a short time when superhero play has disintegrated.
- De-emphasize competition.
- Plan cooperative learning activities.
- Talk with an early childhood consultant. Share pertinent information with the parent(s).
- Add your ideas.

Sample actions parent(s) can take:
- Limit the number of superhero programs your child watches.
- Read books about other things.
- When there is a conflict in a story, stop and figure out a peaceful ending.
- Do things cooperatively, such as make a fruit salad or wash the car.
- Talk with a parent educator or counselor if play is excessively gruesome or violent. Share pertinent information with your provider.
- Add your ideas.

Parent(s) and Provider Action Form

Date:_____

Our plan for _____
                 (CHILD'S NAME)

Goal

Write a realistic goal for this child using one of the examples from this chapter or one of your own.

_____

_____

_____

_____

Actions parent(s) and provider will take

Choose from those in this chapter or use your own ideas.

1. _____
2. _____
3. _____
4. _____

Actions provider will take

Choose from those in this chapter or use your own ideas.

1. _____
2. _____

Actions parent(s) will take

Choose from those in this chapter or use your own ideas.

1. _____
2. _____

We will check in to discuss progress or modify our plan on_____
(set a day six weeks to three months from now).

Signed

_____

(provider)

_____

(parent)

CHAPTER 11

I Want to Play Too: Joining a Group of Players

FOR PROVIDERS

I feel bad when Mackenzie stands on the fringe and watches the others play. One day I watched as she found the toy the others were searching for. She handed it to James and then ran off. It was as if she was scared to join them.

What Is It?

Many children are highly motivated to be a part of group play. Generally, children learn to join the play by watching and copying those in the group. These children join right in and seem readily accepted. Others find it difficult to join already established play groups. They stand on the outskirts and look in or they are excluded from play. When a child appears anxious or as if she does not know how to join in, it is time to intervene. Children need a number of entrance strategies that do not call undue attention to themselves and are not too disruptive. Asking, "Can I play?" is often answered with a resounding, "No!" Adults working with children can help them learn ways to enter play that may be more readily accepted.

Observe and Problem Solve

Ask the following questions as you watch a child having difficulty joining group play. The suggestions that accompany each question will help move this child to a new level of participation.

➤ *Does this child play alone most often?*

It is common for infants, toddlers, and young preschoolers to play alone. Children of all ages play by themselves when they do not know one another very well, are feeling shy, or need some time to themselves. They may also play by themselves because they enjoy it. When children choose to play alone, respect their decision. However, a preschool-aged child could use your help if she appears upset or looks as if she doesn't know how to join in, or if she is always on the outside of play. Encourage interest in materials that support group play such as dramatic play or building with blocks. Offer structured small group activities so that she gets to know others while you are there to direct the activity. Play games that help children learn the names of those in the group. Comment on things that she has in common with others. Say, "You and Kayla both like to pretend about the movie you saw."

➤ *Does this child play well with you or another adult?*

Most children who are successful with their peers have had good relationships with adults. Develop your relationship with this child. Find out what the child enjoys and engage in those activities. Spend time listening to and talking with her. Share a joke or an innocent secret. Learn about her family and what she does outside of your program. Get down on the floor and play with her. Follow her lead, letting her direct the play scenario. When she is able to play well with an adult, help her shift her attention to a child her own age. Look for someone who is similar to her in temperament, interests, and behavior. Choose a slightly younger playmate if you want to boost her confidence and give her practice with leadership skills. Plan paired activities such as fingerpainting, errands, and puppet plays.

Children reject others for many reasons. Some common reasons include:

- To protect a limited number of play materials.
- To protect a role they are enacting.
- To limit the number of players (sometimes, children have difficulty seeing how one more person would fit into the space or story line).
- To feel as if they are a part of a group.
- To feel powerful as they include and exclude players.
- To exclude a newcomer who has a reputation of being disruptive.

Reduce the chances of a newcomer being rejected by helping the child learn entrance strategies that do not call attention to herself or disrupt the play.

1. Teach her to play near the other children and imitate their actions.
2. Join the play yourself and then invite the newcomer in. Help to resolve conflicts.
3. Give the child a prop to bring to the play that supports the story line.
4. Watch to find a role that isn't already taken. Provide the newcomer with ideas about how to act her part.

Remember: Forcing children to include others may build resentment and lead to further rejection.

➤ *Does this child rely on one particular play partner?*

This child may have a best friend who offers support and a friendship in which she is learning many things about trust and intimacy. However, she may have difficulty if her best friend is absent or interested in other people or activities that do not include her. Help her build additional relationships by looking for ways to connect her to new people. Weave her play together with the play of others. If she is cooking and others are making a house, suggest that she take her neighbors some dinner. Join the play yourself, then find ways to include more players. For instance, if you are pretending to go to the movies, include the ticket seller, usher, the person behind the concession stand, as well as the audience.

➤ *Is this child playing on the fringes of the group?*

Help this child imitate the actions of the rest of the group. Draw her attention to what they are doing. Hand her the props she will need. For example, if others are feeding grass to plastic dinosaurs, hand her some grass and suggest she feed hers too. When she has an idea that goes along with the play, help her make her suggestion to another child in the group. Teach her to say the name of one child or get their attention before making her comment. This increases the chances her idea will be acknowledged. She could say, "Rose, let's say the dinosaurs run away from the hot lava."

➤ *Does this child try to join play in a way that is disruptive?*

Help her find a group with which her idea fits. If she wants to play firefighter with children who are rocking babies to sleep, she is likely to be rejected. However, children building with blocks and then knocking them down may take the suggestion more readily.

➤ *Is there an existing activity she would like to join?*

Suggest that she offer a prop that is related to the play. She might bring the coffee to those who are playing house. Or help her join play by pretending to be someone who fits into the play theme. Watch to see that she is not taking a role that someone else has already claimed. Children have difficulty making room for two teachers or two mothers. For instance, if children are playing library, rather than another librarian, suggest that she be the taxi driver who takes people home.

➤ *Does this child use force to try to join others?*

Some children initiate play by slapping a child's shoulder, bulldozing their way into a group, or karate kicking. This aggressive attempt is upsetting to the adults as well as the children; the children will likely reject her. Watch her carefully to see if she is trying to gain entry. Interpret her intentions for others by saying, "I think Lateya is trying to squeeze in this spot to join your game." If this child is aggressive at other times too, teach problem-solving skills (see chapter 15, "Whack! Aggression"). Join the play yourself to help work through difficult situations.

Consider if this child is using physical initiations because her verbal skills are limited. Suggest she take a less verbal role such as the person washing the baby, pretending to be the family pet, or busing dishes at a restaurant. If this child seems stuck using a single approach to join play, encourage her to experiment with a number of different entrance strategies. Offer a suggestion, then add, "If that doesn't work, come back and we'll think of something else." When this child's behavior improves, do not allow children to continue to reject her based on an outgrown aggressive reputation. Talk about the progress she has made toward appropriate behavior.

Work with the Parent(s)

Some people become concerned when a child is not interacting with other children or making friends. They may fondly remember their own childhood friends and want a similar experience for this child. Play with this child for at least a short time each day. Playing with her can help the child learn the relationship skills she needs to play with others. Give the parent(s) the accompanying information and use the Plan for Action to discuss the most useful steps.

When to Get Help

Children who are shy may remain on the outskirts of play for sometime. Watch this child for four to six months before seeking additional help. If a four to four-and-a-half year old who has been in your care for six months still does not engage in play with others, it may be something other than shyness. Consider if this child's language skills are age appropriate. A speech and language specialist can help to assess this child's needs. Other developmental lags such as motor skills that are not yet developed or difficulty understanding pretend play may also cause the child to remain on the outskirts of play. If you believe this child is lagging in development, encourage the parent(s) to take her to their health care provider or an early childhood assessment program in their school district for a developmental screening.

For Further Reading

Hazen, Nancy, Betty Black, and Faye Fleming-Johnson. "Social Acceptance." *Young Children* 39(1984): 26–36.

Heidemann, Sandra, and Deborah Hewitt. *Pathways to Play*. St. Paul: Redleaf Press, 1992.

FOR PARENT(S)

The last few months have been tough for Mackenzie. Every time she tries to play with the other kids in the neighborhood, she comes back crying and says, "They won't let me play." One time I went out to see what was going on and the others said they didn't even know she wanted to play.

What Is It?

Many children are highly motivated to be a part of group play. Generally, children learn to join the play by watching and copying those in the group. These children join right in and seem readily accepted. Others find it difficult to join already established play groups. They stand on the outskirts and look in or they are excluded from play. When a child appears anxious or as if she does not know how to join in, it is time to intervene. Children need a number of entrance strategies that do not call undue attention to themselves and are not too disruptive. Asking, "Can I play?" is often answered with a resounding, "No!" You can help your child learn ways to enter play that may be more readily accepted.

Observe and Problem Solve

Ask the following questions as you watch your child join group play. The suggestions that accompany each question will help move your child to a new level of participation.

➤ *Does your child play alone most often?*

It is common for infants, toddlers, and young preschoolers to play alone. Children of all ages play by themselves when they do not know one another very well, are feeling shy, or need some time to themselves. They may also play by themselves because they enjoy it. When children choose to play alone, respect their decision. However, your preschool-aged child could use your help if she appears upset or looks as if she doesn't know how to join in, or if she is always on the outside of play. Encourage interest in materials that include more than one person in play such as pretend play or building with blocks.

➤ *Does your child play well with you or another adult?*

Most children who are successful with their peers have had good relationships with adults. Include playtime for you and your child each day to be sure she knows play skills. Get down on the floor and play with her. Follow her lead, letting her direct the play scenario. When she is able to play well with you, help her shift her attention to another person. Look for someone who is similar to her in temperament, interests, and behavior. Choose a slightly younger playmate if you want to boost her confidence and give her practice with leadership skills. Invite this child to your home so they will have an opportunity to play while you are there to direct the activity and offer support. Comment on things that she has in common with the playmate. Say, "You and Kayla both like to pretend about the movie you saw."

➤ *Does your child have one best friend?*

Your child may have a regular playmate with whom she plays well. Through this friendship, she may be learning many things about trust and intimacy. This can be a very positive relationship but can leave her upset when her best friend is not around or interested in other people or activities that do not include her. Help her build additional relationships by looking for ways to connect her to new people. Look for others who could be playmates in your neighborhood, early childhood program, or your place of worship. When you have a child in your home for the first time, the visitor will need time to explore. When the children become involved in activities, you may find that they are not playing together. They may be in the same room but using separate materials. Be creative and find ways to weave their play together. If your child is cooking and the other is making a house, suggest that your child take her neighbor some dinner. Join the play yourself to help keep it going and to watch for ways they can play together.

➤ *Is your child playing on the fringes of a group?*

You may not have many opportunities to see your child play with a group of children. Arrange a time to watch her at her early childhood program or take the time to watch as she plays with neighborhood children. Help her learn to be a part of the play. Show her how she can imitate the actions of the rest of the group. Draw her attention to what they are doing. Hand her the props she will need. For example, if others are feeding grass to plastic dinosaurs, hand her some grass and suggest she feed hers too. When she has an idea that goes along with their play, help her make her suggestion to another child. Teach her to say the name of one child or get their attention before making her comment. This increases the chances her idea will be acknowledged. She could say, "Rose, let's say the dinosaurs run away from the hot lava."

➤ *Is there an existing activity your child would like to join?*

Help her watch to see what the group is doing before she tries to join. This way she can decide if she wants to play what they are. If she has a preconceived idea about what to play and tries to take over, she is likely to be rejected. For instance, if children are rocking babies to sleep it will probably not go very well if she insists on playing about a dragon. After watching for a time she can decide to join them or try again later when their ideas better match. If she decides to join the existing activity, suggest that she offer a prop that is related to the play. She might bring the coffee to those who are playing house or offer to be a baby-sitter for those rocking babies to sleep. Watch to see that she is not taking a role that someone else has already claimed. Children have difficulty making room for two teachers or two mothers. For instance, if children are playing library, rather than another librarian, suggest that she be the taxi driver who takes people home.

➤ *Does your child use force to try to join others?*

Some children initiate play by slapping a child's shoulder, bulldozing their way into a group, or karate kicking. This aggressive attempt is upsetting to the other children and they will likely reject her. Watch her carefully to see if she is trying to gain entry. Interpret her intentions for others by saying, "I think Lateya is trying to squeeze into this spot to join your game." If your child is aggressive at other times too, teach problem-solving skills (see chapter 15, "Whack!: Aggression"). Join the play yourself to help work through difficult situations.

Consider if your child is using physical initiations because her verbal skills are limited. Suggest she take a less verbal role such as the person washing the baby, pretending to be the family pet, or busing dishes at a restaurant. If your child seems stuck using a single approach to join play, encourage her to experiment with a number of different entrance strategies. Offer a suggestion, then add, "If that doesn't work, come back and we'll think of something else."

Work with Your Provider

Because your provider sees your child in a group setting, she may be the first to notice the difficulty your child has in joining a group. She may be able to do a number of things in her setting to help your child feel comfortable and encourage group play. At home, you can support your provider's efforts by including daily playtime, inviting other children into your home, and working with your child on appropriate play behaviors. Your provider may be able to make suggestions about playmates who are a good match or those in whom your child takes an interest. Talk with your provider and make a Plan for Action, including the steps that will be taken to teach your child these important relationship skills.

When to Get Help

Children who are shy may remain on the outskirts of play for sometime. If a four to four-and-a-half year old who knows the other children does not engage in group play, her hesitancy, disinterest, or resistance may be something other than shyness. Consider if your child's language skills are age appropriate. A speech and language specialist can help to assess your child's needs. Other developmental lags such as motor skills that are not yet developed or difficulty understanding pretend play may also cause your child to remain on the outskirts of play for an extended period of time. If you suspect that your child is lagging in development, talk to your health care provider or an early childhood assessment program in your school district to schedule a developmental screening.

For Further Reading

Heidemann, Sandra, and Deborah Hewitt. *Pathways to Play*. St. Paul: Redleaf Press, 1992.

A Plan for Action

To develop your Plan for Action, choose a goal that best fits your situation. Then determine three or four actions providers and parent(s) will take. Choose additional actions specific to the early childhood setting and home. Mark your choices on this summary or write them on the planning form that follows.

Sample goals for a child who has difficulty joining group play:
- Plays with an adult.
- Plays with one other child (can be the same child).
- Plays one on one with different children.
- Plays with a group of children (two or more).
- Add your ideas.

Sample actions parent(s) and provider can take:
- Get down on the floor to play with this child each day.
- Follow this child's lead in play.
- Notice and comment on things this child has in common with others.
- Help this child connect with someone who is similar.
- Join the play to facilitate relationships.
- Help this child watch and imitate the play of others.
- Weave this child's play together with that of others.
- Build relationships with more than one child.
- Hand this child props she could bring to the existing play.
- Help this child think of a role that complements what others are doing.
- Teach this child to get the attention of one player before presenting an idea.
- Encourage this child to try a number of entrance strategies.
- Suggest appropriate roles for a child who is less verbal.
- Join the play to coach this child through conflict situations.
- Teach problem-solving skills.
- Interpret this child's actions for others.
- Add your ideas.

Sample actions provider can take:
- Offer materials that support group play.
- Work to develop an adult-child relationship.
- Learn about this child's family and what she likes to do outside of the early childhood program; offer similar experiences.
- Play games that will help this child get to know the other children.
- Offer small group activities lead by the adult.
- Plan paired activities.
- Help this child look for groups to join.
- Teach appropriate play behaviors.
- Comment on improvements in behaviors so others do not reject this child based on an outgrown reputation.
- Add your ideas.

Sample actions parent(s) can take:
- Invite other children to play at your home.
- Direct and support play when children come to your home.
- Arrange for a speech and language screening. Share pertinent information with your provider.
- Arrange for a developmental screening to be done by your health care provider or the early childhood assessment program in your school district. Share pertinent information with your provider.
- Add your ideas.

Parent(s) and Provider Action Form

Date:_____

Our plan for _____
(CHILD'S NAME)

Goal

Write a realistic goal for this child using one of the examples from this chapter or one of your own.

_____

_____

_____

_____

Actions parent(s) and provider will take

Choose from those in this chapter or use your own ideas.

1. _____

2. _____

3. _____

4. _____

Actions provider will take

Choose from those in this chapter or use your own ideas.

1. _____

2. _____

Actions parent(s) will take

Choose from those in this chapter or use your own ideas.

1. _____

2. _____

We will check in to discuss progress or modify our plan on_____

(set a day six weeks to three months from now).

Signed

_____
(provider)

_____
(parent)

CHAPTER 12
It's Mine, Mine, Mine: Turn Taking

Ali sits on the floor, spreads his legs, and dumps a bucket of blocks between them. He never really plays with them. He just keeps guard over them to make sure no one else takes them.

What Is It?

Turn taking wouldn't be a problem if there were enough materials and attention for all the children in a group. However, in most group settings young children are expected to share. Before the age of three and a half or four, many are not developmentally ready to share. Some children hoard materials, refuse to take turns, leave the area when they are required to share, or take things others are using. Learning to share requires a great deal of adult guidance and lots of practice. Children need adults to help them learn to give up materials when they are done with them, ask to play with a material someone else is using, and wait for a turn when there aren't enough things to go around.

Observe and Problem Solve

Watch a child having difficulty learning to share. After you observe, consider the suggestions. Then develop a plan for working with this child.

➤ *Does this child hoard materials and protect them rather than play with them?*

This child may not be ready developmentally to share. He will need many opportunities to have things without being required to take turns.

Make sure you have ample materials and duplicates of those that are favorites. Allow this child plenty of time with a material before asking him to give it up. He must feel as if he has had possession of something before he will willingly share it with others.

Arrange for this child to learn to take turns with you by playing games that have a back and forth rhythm. Roll a car back and forth, bounce a ball to each other, or talk on a toy telephone. Pause expectantly as you wait for the child to return it or take his turn. Emphasize the term "turn" by saying, "Your turn" and "My turn" each time. After practicing with you a number of times, include one other child in your play. Most importantly, lay the groundwork for sharing by being a generous role model.

➤ *Does this child leave a toy, then become upset if someone else uses it?*

Help this child learn that when he leaves a toy others may use it by watching when he changes activities. Go to him and remind him that if he leaves a toy someone else may use it. Let this child control when he passes the toy on to another. Ask him if he is done or if he wants a few more minutes with it. Tell him you can't save it for him (unless he is just going to use the bathroom). Draw a picture of it and let him save the paper. If you must call his turn to an end ask, "Can Tenisha have it now or in two minutes?" When a newcomer joins a group of players, draw attention to her presence. Ask each of the children to give a portion of their materials to the newcomer. Thank the child for whatever he is willing to share, even if it is only a pinch of playdough or a few blocks. Be sure to provide a place for this child to put personal belongings.

➤ *Does this child leave the area, cry, or refuse turn taking?*

Teach this child to take materials that he wants to use by himself to a private area of the room. Identify times of the day when he needs to play alone; steer him toward materials that are typically used by one at a time. Allow children to say to one another, "I want to play alone right now." If he refuses to share, respect his need to control the materials for a time. Do not lecture or reprimand. Help the other child find something of interest. Teach the other child how to know when it is his turn. He can watch for the first child to put toys down or go to another part of the room. Watch to see when the first child leaves the toy. Help the second know it is his turn now.

Comment on times when this child is waiting for a turn, such as waiting for snack or a turn at the drinking fountain. Call attention to daily situations in which people share or those depicted in books or magazines. Notice how happy both parties feel when they share. Practice turn taking and sharing in the dramatic play area by setting up a doctor's waiting room or a bakery with numbers for the customers to take.

A child may worry the toy he is lending will not be returned or will be ruined by the borrower. He may ask to have the toy back right away to see if the other child is trustworthy. Let the child who is giving up the material put some limits on its usage. He could say, "You can look at it if you give it right back." Let him describe how it is to be used by saying something like, "You can use it but don't smash it into any walls."

Structure situations in which turns must be taken. Place chairs at the table to indicate how many children may participate in an activity at one time. Warn children when their turn will be over. Some providers use a timer to let children know their turn is over. Most children seem to make plans for their next activity when this type of warning is provided. Others claim this doesn't allow the child to finish on his own. For those situations in which you are unable to tell who had the material first, use a "turn taker." Cut a circle from cardboard. Put a different color on each side of the circle. One child flips the turn taker; the other calls one of the two colors while it is in the air. If it lands on the color called, it is that child's turn first.

➤ *Does this child ask for adult assistance in turn taking?*

When a child reports that someone has just taken the toy he was using, he is probably asking for help in solving this problem. (See chapter 14, "I'm Telling on You: Tattling" for more information.) Use your professional judgment to determine how much help he needs. If he is new to problem solving, go to the child and help him learn this technique. Describe what you see happening. Say, "It looks like you both want to use this tractor." Ask a "What" question to help them begin to think about ways to solve their problem. Say, "What can you do to work this out?" or "What should you do about that?" or "What can you do that will make you both happy?" Offer a solution if they are unable to come up with one. Say, "One of you can have it first and then it will be the other person's turn." Support others as they try words you model. Prompt those who are capable of problem solving by saying, "Use your words." Comment when you see this child share spontaneously.

➤ *Does this child take things others are using?*

Some children grab materials others are using. Closely supervise a child who has difficulty with this. Try to get to him before a problem occurs. Teach him words he could use. Say, "Thomas is using that. Ask him for a turn. Say, 'Can I have a turn when you are done?'" Help the child find something else to do while waiting. If the waiting period becomes extraordinarily long, help him go back and ask again. He could say, "I've been waiting for a really long time. When will you be done?" Teach this child to make trades. Help him think of something the other child may want and bring it to him.

Watch your own response if you see him take a toy away from another child. Remain calm. If you go to him and take the material he has just taken, you may inadvertently model grabbing. Slow the process down by saying, "Meng was using that." Try the problem-solving strategies mentioned above. If he does not return it, direct him to give it back. Then if need be say, "You need to give it back. Can you do it by yourself or shall I help you?" If he doesn't return the item at this point, you can gently return it.

Confidentially, explain the consequences of taking other's toys (others get angry or may not want to play with you). Put on a puppet play in which two puppets have difficulty sharing. Let the children decide a number of ways the puppets could work out the problem. Act out their solutions and the possible consequences. End with the puppets taking turns.

Work with the Parent(s)

Let the parent(s) know that turn taking is difficult for their child in your setting. They may experience similar problems with turn taking at home. If they do not see the child in a group setting or if he is an only child, they may not see this behavior. Whether or not they have similar concerns, you will want to work with them to develop a Plan for Action. Give them the information for parents and arrange a time to discuss what steps you will take in working with this child. Establishing consistency between home and the early childhood setting will help this child learn appropriate skills more quickly.

When to Get Help

Turn taking is a skill that develops over a number of years. Help this child learn to share. Emphasize the benefits of it. If the child uses aggression to get the materials he wants, see chapter 15, "Whack!: Aggression."

For Further Reading

Heidemann, Sandra, and Deborah Hewitt. *Pathways to Play*. St. Paul: Redleaf Press, 1992.

Oken-Wright, Pam. "From Tug of War to 'Let's Make a Deal': The Teacher's Role." *Young Children* 48(1992): 15–20.

Out of the corner of her eye, Renee saw Michael and Nick grab a large plastic dinosaur at the same time. They looked each other in the eye as they pulled back and forth but no words were exchanged. Renee moved close to the boys. Nick let go of the toy and Michael nearly tumbled over. Renee said, "It looks like you both want the dinosaur." Nick and Michael both insisted they had the dinosaur first. Renee asked, "What could you do so you both get to use the dinosaur?" The boys looked at her without offering any suggestions. Renee proposed that one use it first then the other, but the boys did not respond. Without further participation in discussion, Renee let it drop. The boys abandoned the dinosaur and went to play in the large muscle area.

After this incident, Renee decided she needed to lay the foundation for future problem solving. For the next few days she led group activities to teach problem solving. She did a puppet play with puppets fighting over materials, read books with problems for the children to solve, and used pictures showing conflict as discussion starters.

The next time Renee saw Michael and Nick having trouble sharing, she approached them in the same manner as before. She moved close to them, described what was taking place, and asked, "What could you do about it?" This time they had some ideas. They thought they might share, take turns, or try to find another toy just like the one they wanted. After coming up with these wonderful ideas, they happily ran off without playing with the toy. Maybe next time they would try one of the ideas they had generated.

Ali and his brother are always fighting over toys. Sometimes Ali isn't even interested in a toy until his brother picks it up.

What Is It?

In most families with more than one child, children need to share toys, materials, and adult attention. Before the age of three and a half or four, many are not developmentally ready to do this. Some children hoard materials, refuse to take turns, cry when they are required to share, or take things others are using. Learning to share requires a great deal of adult guidance and lots of practice. Children need adults to help them learn to give up materials when they are done with them, ask to play with a material someone else is using, and wait for a turn when there aren't enough things to go around.

Observe and Problem Solve

Watch your child in situations that require him to share. After you observe, consider the suggestions. Then develop a plan for teaching him to take turns.

➤ *Does your child hoard materials and protect them rather than play with them?*

Your child may not be ready developmentally to share. He will need many opportunities to have things without being required to take turns. Allow him plenty of time with a material before asking him to give it up. He must feel as if he has had possession of something before he will willingly share it with others. Arrange for your child to learn to take turns with you by playing games that have a back and forth rhythm. Roll a car back and forth, bounce a ball to each other, or talk on a toy telephone. Pause expectantly as you wait for your child to return it or take his turn. Emphasize the term "turn" by saying, "Your turn" and "My turn" each time. After practicing with you a number of times, include one other child in your play, if possible. Most importantly, lay the groundwork for sharing by being a generous role model.

➤ *Does your child leave a toy, then become upset if someone else uses it?*

Help your child learn that when he leaves a toy others may use it by watching when he changes activities. Go to him and remind him that if he leaves a toy someone else may use it. Let him control when he passes the toy on to another. Ask him if he is done or if he wants a few more minutes with it. Tell him you can't save it for him (unless he is just going to use the bathroom). If you must call his turn to an end ask, "Can Tenisha have it now or in two minutes?" Before a visitor comes over, ask your child to identify things he doesn't think he can share. Put these things away until after the visitor goes home. Your child may have an easier time sharing when he is at someone else's house since the materials are not his own.

➤ *Does your child cry or refuse turn taking?*

Teach your child to take materials that he wants to use by himself to a private area. Identify times of the day when he needs to play alone and steer him toward solitary play materials (for example, puzzles or reading). Teach your child to say, "I want to play alone right now." If he refuses to share, respect his need to control the materials for a time. Do not lecture or reprimand. Help the other child find something of interest. Teach the other child how to know when it is his turn. He can watch for the first child to put toys down or go to another part of the room. Watch to see when the first child leaves the toy. Help the second know it is his turn now. Comment on times when your child is waiting for a turn, such as waiting for dinner or in the checkout line at the store. Call attention to daily situations in which people share or those depicted in books or magazines. Notice how happy it makes both parties feel when they share. Your child may worry the toy he is lending will not be returned or will be ruined by the borrower. He may ask to have the toy back right away to see if the other child is trustworthy. Let your child put some limits on its usage. He could say, "You can look at it if you give it right back." Let him describe how it is to be used by saying something like, "You can use it but don't smash it into any walls."

Structure situations in which turns must be taken. Warn your child when his turn will be over. Some people use a timer to let children know their turn is over. Most children seem to make plans for their next activity when this type of warning is provided. Others claim this doesn't allow the child to finish on his own.

➤ *Does your child come and tell you when he has trouble taking turns?*

When your child reports that someone has just taken the toy he was using, he is probably asking for help in solving this problem. (See chapter 14, "I'm telling on You: Tattling" for more information.) Determine how much help he needs and how much he can do for himself. If he is new to problem solving, go with your child and help him learn this technique. Describe what you see happening. Say, "It looks like you both want to use the tractor." Ask a "What" question to help the children begin to think about ways to solve their problem. Say, "What can you do to work this out?" or "What should you do about that?" or "What can you do that will make you both happy?" Offer a solution if they are unable to come up with one. Say, "One of you can have it first and then it will be the other person's turn." If your child has some experience problem solving, remind him to ask for a turn. Let him know he can come back for more ideas if his first one does not work. Comment when you see your child share spontaneously.

➤ *Does your child take things others are using?*

Some children grab materials others are using. Closely supervise your child. Try to get to him before a problem occurs. Teach him words he could use. Say, "Thomas is using that. Ask him for a turn. Say, 'Can I have a turn when you are done?'" Help your child find something else to do while waiting. If the waiting period becomes extraordinarily long, help him go back and ask again. He could say, "I've been waiting for a really long time. When will you be done?" Teach your child to make a trade for something he wants. Help him think of something the other child may want and bring it to him.

Watch your own response if you see him take a toy away from another child. Remain calm. If you go to him and take the material he has just taken, you may inadvertently model grabbing. Slow the process down by saying, "Meng was using that. Try the problem-solving strategies mentioned above. If he does not return it, direct him to give it back. Then if need be say, "You need to give it back. Can you do it by yourself or shall I help you?" If he doesn't return the item, you can gently return it. Confidentially, explain the consequences of taking others toys (others get angry or may not want to play with you).

Work with Your Provider

While taking turns may be an area of difficulty for the child at home, it can be magnified in a group setting. When groups of small children come together, it can be difficult for them to share. Talk with your provider to determine what steps you will take in teaching this important skill. Establishing consistency between home and the early childhood setting will help your child learn appropriate skills more quickly.

When to Get Help

Turn taking is a skill that develops over a number of years. Help your child learn to share. Emphasize the benefits of it. If your child uses aggression to get the materials he wants, see chapter 15, "Whack!: Aggression."

For Further Reading

Heidemann, Sandra, and Deborah Hewitt. *Pathways to Play*. St. Paul: Redleaf Press, 1992.

A Plan for Action

To develop your Plan for Action, choose a goal that best fits your situation. Then determine three or four actions providers and parent(s) will take. Choose additional actions specific to the early childhood setting and home. Mark your choices on this summary or write them on the planning form that follows.

Sample goals for a child having difficulty taking turns:
- Takes turns with an adult.
- Leaves a toy and allows others to play with it.
- Takes turns when coached by an adult.
- Asks for a turn.
- Spontaneously takes turns with others.
- Add your ideas.

Sample actions parent(s) and provider can take:
- Be a generous role model.
- Call attention to situations in which people share.
- Describe the benefits of sharing.
- Allow this child plenty of time with a toy.
- Allow this child to play without sharing in a private area.
- Teach this child to say, "I want to play alone."
- Don't lecture or reprimand if this child doesn't share.
- Help the other child find something to do while waiting for a turn.
- Play games that have a back and forth rhythm.
- Include one other child in turn taking games.
- Remind this child someone else may use a toy if he leaves it.
- Warn this child when his turn will be over.
- Allow this child to decide if he will give the toy "Now or in two minutes."
- Move close to this child before turn taking is a problem.

- Structure turn taking for this child.
- Teach this child to describe how something he is lending is to be used.
- Teach this child words to use in asking for a turn.
- Teach this child to make trades.
- Help this child problem solve.
- Ask a "what" question to aid in problem solving.
- Comment when this child shares spontaneously.
- Add your ideas.

Sample actions provider can take:
- Provide plenty of materials.
- Provide a place for personal belongings.
- Buy duplicates of favorite materials.
- Put on a puppet play about turn taking.
- Practice turn taking in dramatic play situations.
- When someone joins a group and materials must be divided, let this child decide how much he will share.
- Draw a picture of a toy or project to "save" it.
- Use a "turn taker."
- Add your ideas.

Sample actions parent(s) can take:
- Ask this child to identify things he is not able to share with a visitor. Put these away.
- Add your ideas.

Parent(s) and Provider Action Form

Date:_____

Our plan for _____
         (CHILD'S NAME)

Goal

Write a realistic goal for this child using one of the examples from this chapter or one of your own.

_____

_____

_____

_____

Actions parent(s) and provider will take

Choose from those in this chapter or use your own ideas.

1. _____
2. _____
3. _____
4. _____

Actions provider will take

Choose from those in this chapter or use your own ideas.

1. _____
2. _____

Actions parent(s) will take

Choose from those in this chapter or use your own ideas.

1. _____
2. _____

We will check in to discuss progress or modify our plan on_____
(set a day six weeks to three months from now).

Signed

_____

(provider)

_____

(parent)

CHAPTER 13

##@&!!
Inappropriate Language and Swearing

Kaelyn has been using a lot of foul language lately. The worst part is she knows how to use it. Some of the other children are copying her. I've even had a parent complain about it.

What Is It?

Children sometimes use inappropriate language. Many use swear words without knowing what they mean. They learn these words from other children, brothers and sisters, parents, and the media. Although they may not understand what they are saying, they usually have a sense that these words are not a part of pleasant conversation. Many children, especially four year olds, seem to enjoy this kind of out-of-bounds talk. Adults hearing a young child talk like this usually react in one of two ways: with laughter or shock. The child may enjoy being able to elicit either response and may try to arrive at the same results through continued use of the words. Adults working with young children must help them learn this type of language is not to be used and teach them other ways to express themselves.

Observe and Problem Solve

Observe the child who is using inappropriate language. Find out when she swears and if possible why it continues. This will help you determine how to curb it.

➤ *Is this child imitating others who swear?*

Children imitate the things they see and hear. They try out inappropriate words they have heard because it makes them feel grown-up or powerful and because it gets a reaction. Deal with swearing or foul language when you first hear it. If you ignore it completely, you may unintentionally give the message that using that language is okay. Respond in a matter-of-fact manner. Make it clear that swearing is not acceptable in your setting. Say, "That's a word we don't use here." Distract this child to a more appropriate activity. Children repeat what you say, so model the kind of language you want to hear. The child who swears immediately after someone else needs to learn better ways to get attention. Whisper to her, "You have good ideas of your own. You don't need to copy Josh's words." Sometimes children are being silly or experimenting with language and happen on unacceptable words. Help this child continue her fun with sounds by making up silly or rhyming words. You could say, "What rhymes with crackle? pow? padiddle?"

➤ *Is this child part of a group in which swearing is acceptable?*

If swearing is acceptable in this child's home or the group of children with whom this child socializes, it may be difficult to eliminate all swearing. Decrease swearing in your setting by focusing on teaching this child more acceptable words to use. Talk with this child confidentially. Say, "That sounds like something a grown-up might say. It's not okay to say that here." Do not talk negatively about the setting in which it is used. Accept differences while clearly stating the expectations for your setting. Let her know of some of the consequences for continuing to use this type of language: it upsets other people; others may not want to be around her when she

109

talks like that; she may be embarrassed if she says that in front of some people (like her grandmother or a teacher).

➤ *Are other children provoking her? Is an activity causing upset or frustration?*

Watch this child to determine when she is becoming upset. Her face may become flushed; her voice may get louder, higher in pitch, or change in quality (that is, become whiny); and more arguments over toys may start. Intervene before she is so frustrated that she swears. Give her ideas about how she can handle her frustration. She can get an adult, leave the area, or say, "This is too hard for me." Reduce competition in activities or the level of difficulty so she feels more successful. Lower your expectations for this child. If she is becoming frustrated, offer your support. Recognize that she has attempted a difficult or complicated task. Help her with it.

➤ *Is this child swearing to express anger or other negative emotions?*

For children who have been aggressive when angry, using words is an improvement, even if the words are inappropriate by most standards. Make sure this child knows you do not like swearing. Teach this child to deal with her frustration in other ways. She could get help, walk away, or use problem-solving techniques. Give her words to use when she is angry. Say, "I know you are angry. You can tell me 'I'm so mad.'" Replace swear words with those that are more acceptable like "shoot" or "oh my goodness." Expand the vocabulary of words she uses to express feelings. Include a range from "upset" to "furious." Look at magazines and books to see what the people who are pictured might be feeling and why. If a problem is pictured, think with this child about possible solutions.

If it is necessary for this child to leave an upsetting activity for a short time, require her to choose a quiet activity to do by herself. When she is in control of her emotions, she can rejoin the others. You will probably need to assist with this reunion in order for it to be successful.

➤ *What happens after this child swears? Does this child look at you, say the offensive word, and then wait for a response?*

Often, a child receives a great deal of attention for swearing, whether it be laughter or lecture. The attention that keeps the behavior going may come from you, the other children, or from outside your setting. You may not be able to do anything about the attention this child receives for swearing in other places, but you can reduce the amount she receives when she is in your care. Increase the amount of positive attention this child receives at other times. Make a point of going to this child early in the day and often. Talk with her and pay attention to her when she is being appropriate. Point out positive things about this child in front of other children. Say something like, "Kaelyn is really creative when she paints." If she does swear, keep a straight face as you put the suggestions listed in this chapter into effect (for more information on attention getting, see chapter 5, "Watch This!: Attention Getting").

If one child reports that another is using inappropriate language, tell them to let the child know they don't like this. Let the child who reports know that he can move away from the child who is swearing. Help the other children refocus their attention.

Work with the Parent(s)

There are many people and places that children hear swearing. Only one source is the parent. Do not assume that the parent is permitting swearing or modeling it. Most parents use appropriate language in front of their children. Occasionally a swear word will slip out and this may be the one word the child imitates. It can be frustrating when the child repeats many times the one word said by mistake. Some parents use this type of language as a way to express themselves.

Whether it is the occasional word, typical language for a parent, or learned from someone else, talk with the parent and let them know their child is swearing. Give them the information for parents and meet to discuss your Plan for Action. Establishing consistency between home and the early childhood setting will help this child learn appropriate behavior more quickly.

When to Get Help

If swearing does not decrease after three to four months despite your efforts to reduce it, this child may not understand this rule or others you have. If the child is having difficulty understanding all types of rules, have this child screened to see if her skills are developing at an age appropriate rate. If she expresses anger that seems out of proportion to the situation, or if the anger is prompted by a chronic stressor in this child's life, suggest that the parent(s) talk with a family counselor to help her learn coping strategies.

For Further Reading

Gartrell, Daniel. "Punishment or Guidance?" *Young Children* 42(1987): 55–61.

McCarney, Stephen, and Angela Bauer. *The Parent's Guide*. Columbia, MO: Hawthorne Educational Services, 1989.

I couldn't believe it the first time Kaelyn swore. My mouth dropped to the floor. I don't know where she had heard words like that.

What Is It?

Children sometimes use inappropriate language. Many use swear words without knowing what they mean. They learn the words from other children, brothers and sisters, adults, and the media. Although they may not understand what they are saying, they usually have a sense that these words are not a part of pleasant conversation. Many children, especially four year olds, seem to enjoy this kind of out-of-bounds talk. Adults hearing a young child talk like this usually react in one of two ways: with laughter or shock. The child may enjoy being able to elicit either response and may try to arrive at the same results through continued use of the words. If your child tries out these words, you can help her learn this type of language is not to be used and teach her other ways to express herself.

Observe and Problem Solve

Observe your child. Find out when she swears and if possible why it continues. This will help you determine how to curb it.

➤ *Is your child imitating others who swear?*

Children imitate the things they see and hear. They try out inappropriate words they have heard because it makes them feel grown-up or powerful, or because it gets a reaction. Deal with swearing or foul language when you first hear it. If you ignore it completely, you may unintentionally give the message that using that language is okay. Respond in a matter-of-fact manner. Make it clear that swearing is not acceptable. Say, "That's a word we don't use." Distract your child to a more appropriate activity. Children repeat what you say, so model the kind of language you want to hear. Monitor the television programs your child watches to ensure they use appropriate language. The child who swears

immediately after someone else needs to learn better ways to get attention. Whisper to her, "You have good ideas of your own. You don't need to copy Josh's words." Sometimes children are being silly or experimenting with language and happen on unacceptable words. Help your child continue her fun with sounds by making up silly or rhyming words. You could say, "What rhymes with crackle? pow? padiddle?"

➤ *Is this child part of a group in which swearing is acceptable?*

If swearing is acceptable in the group of children with whom she socializes, it may be difficult to eliminate all swearing. Decrease swearing in front of you by focusing on teaching your child more acceptable words to use. Talk with her confidentially. Say, "That sounds like something a grown-up might say. It's not okay to say that word." Find ways to let her socialize with people who do not use swearing as a part of conversation. Let your child know some of the consequences for continuing to use this type of language: it upsets other people; others may not want to be around her when she talks like that; she may be embarrassed if she says that in front of others (like her grandmother or a teacher).

➤ *Are other children provoking her? Is an activity causing upset or frustration?*

Watch your child to determine when she is becoming upset. Her face may become flushed; her voice may get louder, higher in pitch, or change in quality (that is, become whiny); and more arguments over toys may start. Intervene before she is so frustrated that she swears. Give her ideas about how she can handle her frustration. She can get an adult, leave the area, or say, "This is too hard for me." Reduce competition in activities or the level of difficulty so she feels more successful. If she is becoming frustrated, offer your support. Recognize that she has attempted a difficult or complicated task. Help her with it.

➤ *Is this child swearing to express anger or other negative emotions?*

For children who have been aggressive when angry, using words is an improvement, even if the words are inappropriate by most standards.

Make sure your child knows you do not like swearing. Teach her to deal with her frustration in other ways. She could get help, walk away, or use problem solving techniques. Give her words to use when she is angry. Say, "I know you are angry. You can tell me 'I'm so mad.'" Replace swear words with those that are more acceptable like "shoot" or "oh my goodness." Expand the vocabulary of words she uses to express feelings. Include a range from "upset" to "furious." Look at magazines and books to see what the people who are pictured might be feeling and why. If a problem is pictured, think with your child about possible solutions.

If it is necessary for your child to leave an upsetting activity for a short time, require her to choose a quiet activity to do by herself. When she is in control of her emotions, she can rejoin the others. You will probably need to assist with this reunion in order for it to be successful.

➤ *What happens after your child swears? Does she look at you, say the offensive word, and then wait for a response?*

Often, a child receives a great deal of attention for swearing, whether it be laughter or lecture. The attention that keeps the behavior going may come from you, other children, or from another setting. You may not be able to do anything about the attention your child receives for swearing in other places, but you can reduce the amount she receives when she is at home. Increase the amount of positive attention she receives at other times. Make a point of talking with her and paying attention to her when she is behaving appropriately. If she does swear, keep a straight face as you put the suggestions listed in this chapter into effect (for more information on attention getting, see chapter 5, "Watch This! Attention Getting").

Work with Your Provider

There are many places that children hear swearing. An early childhood setting may be one of them. Talk with your provider about decreasing its occurrence. Develop a Plan for Action. Work to establish consistency between home and the early childhood setting to teach your child more acceptable behavior.

For Parents and Providers: Signs a Child Is Becoming Frustrated or Upset

- voice becomes louder
- voice changes in pitch and quality (whining)
- speaks more quickly
- face becomes flushed
- arguments erupt
- two hold onto or grab for the same toy at the same time

Adapted from *Pathways to Play* by Sandra Heidemann and Deborah Hewitt. St. Paul: Redleaf Press, 1992. Used with permission.

When to Get Help

If swearing does not decrease after three to four months despite your efforts to reduce it, your child may not understand this rule or others. If your child is having difficulty understanding all types of rules, have her skills screened to see if she is developing skills at an age appropriate rate. Contact your school district or an early childhood education program in your area. If she expresses anger that seems out of proportion to the situation, or if the anger is prompted by a chronic stressor in your child's life, talk with a family counselor who can help her learn coping strategies.

For Further Reading

Gartrell, Daniel. "Punishment or Guidance?" *Young Children* 42(1987): 55–61.

McCarney, Stephen, and Angela Bauer. *The Parent's Guide*. Columbia, MO: Hawthorne Educational Services, 1989.

A Plan for Action

To develop your Plan for Action, choose a goal that best fits your situation. Then determine three or four actions providers and parent(s) will take. Choose additional actions specific to the early childhood setting and home. Mark your choices on this summary or write them on the planning form that follows.

Sample goals for a child who swears:
- Increases frustration tolerance.
- Uses appropriate words to express anger and frustration.
- Seeks attention in appropriate ways.
- Add your ideas.

Sample actions parent(s) and provider can take:
- Model appropriate language.
- Allow fun with sounds through silly rhymes.
- Respond in a matter-of-fact manner when this child swears.
- Make it clear swearing is not acceptable.
- Distract to a more appropriate activity.
- Intervene before a child who swears gets frustrated.
- Help this child with difficult tasks.
- Expand her vocabulary of words to use to express feelings.
- Replace swear words with "shoot" or "nuts."
- Praise this child for controlling her anger.
- Talk with this child about the consequences of continued swearing (for example, loss of friends, embarrassment).
- Have this child choose a quiet activity if she must leave an upsetting activity for a short time.
- Add your ideas.

Sample actions provider can take:
- Point out positive things about this child in front of others.
- Reduce competition.
- Add your ideas.

Sample actions parent(s) can take:
- Monitor television programs your child watches.
- Encourage friendships with people who do not swear.
- Arrange for your health care provider or the early childhood assessment program in your school district to conduct a developmental screening. Share pertinent information with your provider.
- Talk with a family counselor. Share pertinent information with your provider.
- Add your ideas.

Parent(s) and Provider Action Form

Date:_____

Our plan for _____
                   (CHILD'S NAME)

Goal

Write a realistic goal for this child using one of the examples from this chapter or one of your own.

_____

_____

_____

_____

Actions parent(s) and provider will take

Choose from those in this chapter or use your own ideas.

1. _____

2. _____

3. _____

4. _____

Actions provider will take

Choose from those in this chapter or use your own ideas.

1. _____

2. _____

Actions parent(s) will take

Choose from those in this chapter or use your own ideas.

1. _____

2. _____

We will check in to discuss progress or modify our plan on_____

(set a day six weeks to three months from now).

Signed

_____

(provider)

_____

(parent)

CHAPTER 14

I'm Telling on You: Tattling

Isaiah tells on everybody. He doesn't even try to take care of it himself.

What Is It?

Reporting on the behavior of others, complaining about their actions, drawing attention to rule infractions, and telling about another person's wrong doings are considered "tattling" and are usually discouraged. Adults frown on tattling because they view it as attending to someone else's business; they are concerned that the child who tattles will lose friends. Children also oppose tattling, seeing it as disloyal and weak. Words such as "tattletale," "snitch," "stool pigeon," or "rat" suggest the negative attitudes toward this behavior.

Children today are faced with many difficult challenges. Traditional responses to tattling, such as ignoring it or turning children away, are no longer appropriate. Children must feel free to tell trusted adults when someone is hurting or bothering them or when someone is in danger. When they are older, children must feel free to tell adults when someone is using drugs or carrying a weapon. Adults need to begin to change the connotation of reporting and recognize that in many situations telling an adult is the right thing to do. Adults need to handle the serious situations children face. In most cases of reporting, however, a young child can be taught to handle problems independently. With problem-solving skills, the need to report should decrease.

Observe and Problem Solve

Many adults believe the reason a child tattles is to get another into trouble. While this may be one motivation, other reasons exist as well. Watch the child who tattles frequently. Ask the following questions and consider what reason the child may have for reporting. Then think about how you will tailor your responses to fit each situation.

➤ *Does this child tell on others in order to draw attention to himself?*

Sometimes adults deal with reporting by distracting the child to another activity; contradicting what the child is saying by answering, "She wouldn't do that"; or lecturing about the consequences of tattling. These responses give the child a lot of attention and may reinforce tattling. Instead, listen to what this child has to tell you. Decide if his complaint is reasonable. Determine if he has the skills to handle the situation for himself. If so, send him back to cope with it. If not, provide alternatives for him to try. Consider if this child seeks attention in other ways as well. Prevent the need for getting attention through tattling by giving him plenty of attention at other times. Spend a few minutes with this child early each day. Talk with this child often about subjects in which he is interested.

➤ *Is this child telling you about behaviors of others because you sometimes want to know?*

Many times an adult asks an older child to help look after younger ones. The older child may feel a sense of responsibility to tell an adult if something that is not permitted is taking place. Avoid giving mixed messages. Allow this child to tell you, but let him know that, unless you ask, he doesn't need to be in charge. Say, "Thanks for telling me" or "I know."

➤ *Does this child appear nervous about the actions of others or concerned for their safety?*

In some cases, you may be grateful to this child for bringing a dangerous situation to your attention. Other times, you may be aware of what is taking place. Reassure this child by saying, "Yes, I'm watching. She is climbing very high, isn't she?" Having had adult contact and knowing that you are attending may be enough to reduce the child's fear and allow him to return to his own play. If this type of reporting is persistent, you might add, "It's my job to keep her safe and it's your job to play."

➤ *Does this child tell about rule infractions as if to see if the rules are the same for all or if rules will be enforced?*

Reassure this child that you will take care of a problem if needed. Be consistent in your rules and consequences for them. Sometimes a child is looking for affirmation that he knows and follows the rules. Acknowledge his comment by saying, "I'm glad you know the rules."

➤ *Has this child tried to resolve the situation on his own but has been unsuccessful?*

Children will seek adult backing to make their words work and help them to get what they want. Let this child tell you about the situation. Paraphrase what he says. This gives him the chance to tell you more and to correct any misunderstandings you may have. Let him know you believe he can manage by asking, "What could you do?" This may be all he needs to go back and try again. If he needs help, give alternatives such as, "How about letting him play with one of your old dolls?" If the child still seems unsure of himself, offer to go with him as he works to solve the problem. Your presence will inspire confidence and show your support for him.

➤ *Does this child tell on others in order to make himself look better? Does he try to look like "the good one" by pointing out the misdeeds of others?*

Start by building this child's self-esteem at times when he is not telling on others. Comment on his competencies and let him know his importance. When he is reporting, acknowledge his comments in a noncommittal way by saying, "Oh" or "I'm sorry you're not getting along." Give this child the confidence that he can manage the situation on his own. Say, "You're very good at figuring out ways to include others. I'm sure you'll find a way to work this out."

➤ *Does this child tell on others in order to get them into trouble or for power?*

You might overhear this child say, "I'm going to tell!" as a way to enhance his power and stop an unwanted action. Avoid rushing in to be the enforcer or to solve a problem for him. Listen to what he has to say but give the responsibility to resolve the situation to the child. If the dispute is about sharing ask, "What can you do to get your toy back?" Help him decide which solutions are the best and which are unacceptable by asking, "What would happen if you did that?" If he is unable to think of anything to do, make two suggestions. Say, "Try making a trade for another toy he likes. If that doesn't work, come back and we'll think of something else." When children are just learning to solve conflicts, they need help thinking of a number of different strategies. They also need to know that they can experiment with strategies and that they may need to try more than one. Of course, there are also situations in which the lesson to be learned is to cope when you don't get your own way. If this child is unable to solve the problem on his

---

Reasons a Child May Tattle

- He is worried about the actions of another child.

- He is seeking affirmation or praise for staying within the rules.

- He has been unsuccessful in solving a problem on his own.

- He wants to call attention to himself.

- He thinks you want to know.

- He is trying to "look good."

- He seems to want to get another child "in trouble."

own, act as a mediator. Hold a meeting in which both children tell you their side of what is taking place. After listening to each ask, "What can you do to work it out so you are both happy?" They may need help with ideas at first, but eventually they will become skilled at thinking of solutions.

Work with the Parent(s)

Talk with the child's parent(s) about the importance of allowing children to be able to tell adults anything. Share examples of problems this child brought to you but then solved on his own as well as those he was unable to solve. Anticipate the types of situations in which he may need help and how you will both respond. Discuss with them the Plan for Action. Establishing this type of consistency between home and the early childhood setting will help him get the message that he can tell adults anything and you will help him learn to handle situations independently.

When to Get Help

When tattling is persistent despite your efforts, observe again. Look to see if this child is having difficulty interacting competently or fitting into the group. If he is, work with him on social skills that are essential to successful group play. See chapter 11, "I Want to Play Too: Joining a Group of Players," and the suggested readings for further information.

For Further Reading

Heidemann, Sandra, and Deborah Hewitt. *Pathways to Play*. St. Paul: Redleaf Press, 1992.

Katz, Lilian. "The Professional Early Childhood Teacher." *Young Children* 39(1984): 3–10.

Saifer, Steffen. *Practical Solutions to Practically Every Problem*. St. Paul: Redleaf Press, 1990.

Everybody tells me to just ignore Isaiah's tattling, but it isn't getting any better. He tells on his sister for every little thing.

What Is It?

Reporting on the behavior of others, complaining about their actions, drawing attention to rule infractions, and telling about another person's wrong doings are considered "tattling" and are usually discouraged. Adults frown on tattling because they view it as attending to someone else's business; they are concerned that the child who tattles will lose friends. Children also oppose tattling, seeing it as disloyal and weak. Words like "tattletale," "snitch," "stool pigeon," or "rat" suggest the negative attitudes toward this behavior.

Children today are faced with many difficult challenges. Traditional responses to tattling, such as ignoring it or turning children away, are no longer appropriate. Children must feel free to tell trusted adults when someone is hurting or bothering them or when someone is in danger. When they are older, children must feel free to tell adults when someone is using drugs or carrying a weapon. Adults need to begin to change the connotation of reporting and recognize that in many situations telling an adult is the right thing to do. Adults need to handle the serious situations children face. Although complaining and reporting can be frustrating, effective responses can help children learn to talk with adults about their problems and how to solve them.

Observe and Problem Solve

Many adults believe the reason a child tattles is to get another into trouble. While this may be one motivation, other reasons exist as well. Watch your child during play. Ask the following questions and consider what reasons your child may have for reporting. Then think about how you will tailor your responses to fit each situation.

➤ *Does your child tell on others in order to draw attention to himself?*

Sometimes adults deal with reporting by distracting the child to another activity; contradicting what the child is saying by answering, "She wouldn't do that"; or lecturing about the consequences of tattling. These responses give the child a lot of attention and may reinforce tattling. Instead, listen to what your child has to tell you. Decide if his complaint is reasonable. Determine if he has the skills to handle the situation for himself. If so, send him back to cope with it. If not, provide alternatives for him to try. Consider if your child seeks attention in other ways as well. Prevent the need for getting attention through tattling by giving him plenty of attention at other times. Spend time together each day.

➤ *Is your child telling you about behaviors of others because you sometimes want to know?*

Many times an older child is asked to help look after a younger one and parents expect to know what is taking place. Your child may feel a sense of responsibility to tell you if something that is not permitted is taking place. Avoid giving mixed messages. Allow your child to tell you, but let him know that, unless you ask, he doesn't need to be in charge. Say, "Thanks for telling me," or "I know."

➤ *Does your child appear nervous about the actions of others or concerned for their safety?*

In some cases, you may be grateful to your child for bringing a dangerous situation to your attention. Other times, you may be aware of what is taking place. Reassure your child by saying, "Yes, I'm watching. She is climbing very high, isn't she?" Having had adult contact and knowing that you are attending may be enough to reduce your child's fear and allow him to return to his own play. If this type of reporting is persistent, you might add, "I'll help keep her safe and you can play."

➤ *Does your child tell about rule infractions as if to see if the rules are the same for all or if rules will be enforced?*

Reassure your child that you will take care of a problem if needed. Be consistent in your rules

Children need to feel free to tell a trusted adult anything that is concerning them. For those times when someone's safety may be at risk, it is especially important for a child to tell a grown-up what is taking place. These times may include:

- when people are getting hurt
- if someone is hurting the child and he is unable to stop that person
- if the child is being touched in ways that make him feel uncomfortable
- when the child knows someone is using drugs
- when the child knows someone is carrying a weapon.

and consequences for them. If your child is looking for affirmation that he knows and follows the rules, acknowledge his comment by saying "I'm glad you know the rules."

➤ *Has your child tried to resolve the situation on his own but has been unsuccessful?*

Children will seek adult backing to make their words work and help them get what they want. Let your child tell you about the situation. Paraphrase what he says. This gives him the chance to tell you more and to correct any misunderstandings you may have. Let him know you believe he can manage by asking, "What could you do?" This may be all he needs to go back and try again. If he needs help, give alternatives such as, "How about letting him play with one of your old dolls?" If the child still seems unsure of himself, offer to go with him as he works to solve the problem. Your presence will inspire confidence and show your support for him.

➤ *Does your child tell on others in order to make himself look better? Does he try to look like "the good one" by pointing out the misdeeds of others?*

Start by building your child's self-esteem at times when he is not telling on others. Comment on his competencies and let him know how important he is to you. When he is reporting, acknowledge his comments in a noncommittal way by saying, "Oh" or "I'm sorry you're not getting

along." Give your child confidence that he can manage the situation on his own. Say, "You're very good at figuring out ways your brother can play with you. I'm sure you'll find a way to include him."

➤ *Does your child tell on others in order to get them into trouble or for power?*

You might overhear your child say, "I'm going to tell!" as a way to enhance his power and stop an unwanted action. Avoid rushing in to be the enforcer or to solve a problem for him. Listen to what he has to say but give the responsibility to resolve the situation to your child. Ask, "What can you do to get your toy back?" Help him decide which solutions are best and which are unacceptable by asking, "What would happen if you did that?" If he is unable to think of anything to do, make two suggestions. If the dispute is about sharing say, "Try making a trade for another toy he likes. If that doesn't work come back and we'll think of something else." When children are just learning to solve conflicts, they need help thinking of a number of different strategies. They also need to know that they can experiment with strategies and that they may need to try more than one. Of course, there are also situations in which the lesson to be learned is to cope when you won't get your own way.

If your child is unable to solve the problem on his own, act as a mediator. Hold a meeting in which both children tell you their side of what is taking place. After listening to each ask, "What can you do to work it out so you are both happy?" They may need help with ideas at first, but eventually they will become skilled at thinking of solutions.

Work with Your Provider

Talk with your provider about the importance of allowing children to tell adults anything. Share examples of problems your child brought to you but then solved on his own as well as those he was not able to solve. Anticipate the types of situations in which he may need help and how you will both respond. Develop a Plan for Action. Establishing this type of consistency between home and your early childhood setting will help him get the message that he can tell adults anything and you will help him learn to handle situations independently.

When to Get Help

When tattling is persistent despite your efforts, observe again. Look to see if your child is having difficulty interacting with others competently. If he is, work with him on play and social skills that are essential to successful group play. See chapter 11, "I Want to Play Too: Joining a Group of Players," and the suggested readings for further information.

For Further Reading

Heidemann, Sandra, and Deborah Hewitt. *Pathways to Play*. St. Paul: Redleaf Press, 1992.

Saifer, Steffen. *Practical Solutions to Practically Every Problem*. St. Paul: Redleaf Press, 1990.

A Plan for Action

To develop your Plan for Action, choose a goal that best fits your situation. Then determine three or four actions providers and parent(s) will take. Choose additional actions specific to the early childhood setting and home. Mark your choices on this summary or write them on the planning form that follows.

Sample goals for a child who reports on the behavior of others:

- Asks for attention in appropriate ways.
- Is responsible for his own actions (knows you will take care of other situations).
- Uses words to solve problems.
- Experiments with more than one solution to a problem.
- Seeks assistance when problem-solving efforts don't work.
- Add your ideas.

Sample actions parent(s) and provider can take:

- Comment on this child's competencies.
- Be consistent in rules and consequences.
- Affirm this child when he is following rules.
- Listen to complaints and reports.
- Tailor responses to fit each situation.
- Reassure this child you are aware of what is taking place.
- Paraphrase what this child says when he complains.
- Provide ideas about ways this child can handle a situation that concerns him.
- Encourage experimentation with more than one problem-solving strategy.

- Offer to go with this child as he tries to work out a problem.
- Give the responsibility for solving the problem to this child.
- Give this child confidence that he can manage the situation on his own.
- Avoid rushing in to be the enforcer or to solve the problem for him.
- Act as a mediator in disputes; listen to both sides.
- Acknowledge this child's complaints in a non-committal way.
- Add your ideas.

Sample actions provider can take:

- Let this child know he doesn't need to be in charge unless you ask.
- Add your ideas.

Sample actions parent(s) can take:

- Avoid asking this child to be responsible at certain times but not others.
- Add your ideas.

Parent(s) and Provider Action Form

Date:_____

Our plan for _____
                    (CHILD'S NAME)

Goal

Write a realistic goal for this child using one of the examples from this chapter or one of your own.

_____

_____

_____

_____

Actions parent(s) and provider will take

Choose from those in this chapter or use your own ideas.

1. _____
2. _____
3. _____
4. _____

Actions provider will take

Choose from those in this chapter or use your own ideas.

1. _____
2. _____

Actions parent(s) will take

Choose from those in this chapter or use your own ideas.

1. _____
2. _____

We will check in to discuss progress or modify our plan on_____

(set a day six weeks to three months from now).

Signed

_____

(provider)

_____

(parent)

CHAPTER 15

Whack! Aggression

FOR PROVIDERS

I've got to watch Courtney all the time. Anytime she doesn't get the toy she wants, she hits whoever is playing with it.

What Is It?

Aggressive behaviors cause a great deal of disruption and concern for providers. Typically, aggressive behaviors are those that injure people or property. Hitting, kicking, slapping, pulling hair, pinching, scratching, and biting are all aggressive behaviors. Biting seems to be extremely upsetting to those involved and is discussed separately in chapter 16, "Chomp!: Biting."

Unfortunately, aggressive behaviors can be common to programs with young children because the children have not yet learned to express their strong emotions in more appropriate ways. When children come together in group settings, they are more likely to experience frustration and conflict that can cause aggression. Occasionally, children will demonstrate aggressive behaviors in a group setting but not at home. More typically, children use these behaviors in response to frustration in any setting.

Observe and Problem Solve

Knowing that aggression can be common doesn't make it easier to deal with. Observe the situations in which a child may become aggressive. The following questions and suggestions will help as you formulate your plans.

➤ *Is the child trying to make contact with someone in an inappropriate manner? Is she trying to be friendly?*

Teach ways to touch that do not involve pushing or shoving. Children can shake hands and rub or pat their friend's back. Notice when this child is being friendly and using a gentle touch. Help her learn to greet another child or ask her to play by offering an appealing play idea. (For more information on initiating play with others, see chapter 11, "I Want to Play Too: Joining a Group of Players.")

➤ *Does this child need more space?*

Some children have difficulty keeping their hands to themselves when they are seated next to each other at group activities or snack time. Make sure there is adequate space between individuals. Define personal space with a carpet square, tape mark on the floor, or chair. Separate those that have the most difficulty. Assign seats if need be. Teach this child and her neighbor to say "move over." Be well prepared so this child won't have to wait too long. Give her something to hold or manipulate.

➤ *Was a behavior misinterpreted and thought to be aggressive?*

When children are crowded, they are likely to bump into one another or knock things over. Children who are aggressive often misinterpret accidents as aggression. Further aggression follows when the second child retaliates. You may need to quickly describe the situation as accidental. Say something like, "Sarah accidentally knocked down your blocks when she tried to get to her building. If you build farther over here it may not happen." Avoid the situation altogether by making sure each child has enough room to play.

Other situations in which children misinterpret contact might be bumping into one another in line, pushing (tagging) when trying to join a game of tag, or trying to make space for themselves. Help reinterpret the situation by saying something like, "Roshaan pushed you over because he wants to sit on the spot next to you." Consider if this child has difficulty understanding other aspects of play. A child who does not catch on to social feedback or does not comprehend complicated pretend play may become frustrated and strike out.

➤ *How much language is this child using?*

A child who uses very few words or who is difficult to understand is more likely to respond to a conflict with aggressive behavior. You can help her learn words to use in the situation, come and get you for help, or even yell rather than hit. Once you are aware of the conflict, you can help by offering words she can use. Keep these words very simple. "Stop," "That's mine," or "Help" are examples. When this child is ready, teach more complex statements like, "I was using that" or "When can I have a turn?" Give her lots of positive attention for using words instead of hitting. If you can get to her before she is aggressive, tell her gently but firmly that she needs to use words.

➤ *Is this child trying to engage another in roly-poly play? Has roly-poly play turned aggressive?*

Many children love to roll around and physically engage in play with others. To help meet this need, provide indoor and outdoor movement opportunities each day. Consider having a gym mat on which children can wrestle. Set limits when children use it, including stop when someone says "Stop," only two children at a time, only wrestling, and a grown-up must supervise. Help her get involved in another activity after this type of play. Try sensory experiences like playdough, water, sand, and fingerpainting with shaving cream. Give opportunities for this child to be powerful in other ways by having her help to make rules, run errands, and plan activities. Comment on times she uses "her strong muscles" to help rearrange furniture or climb to the top of the playground equipment.

➤ *Is this child using aggression to express anger or to get what she wants?*

Teach a child who is aggressive when angry to express herself in other ways. Safe ways include telling someone, yelling, stamping feet, pounding playdough, or scribbling on a piece of paper. Model the use of words to express your own feelings of anger.

Be clear that aggression will not be permitted. Say, "I won't let you hit others. Hitting hurts." Direct children through conflict situations by saying, "Troy was using that. You need to give the toy back. Ask him to give it to you when he is done with it." Older preschool children can begin to learn problem-solving skills. Help them to identify the problem, brainstorm solutions, pick one to try, and evaluate how it worked. Problem-solving meetings can help everyone calm down. Ask each child what happened. Then get problem solving started by asking, "What can you do that will make both of you happy?" If they are unable to come up with any solutions, suggest a few for them. Read books in which a problem is presented (such as those in Elizabeth Crary's *Children's Problem Solving Series*). Discuss how the problem could be solved.

➤ *Is this child hitting many times per day or for a number of months?*

If the child has persistent difficulty controlling her aggression, a concerted effort to reduce this behavior may be needed. Teach this child to recognize when she is angry, stop and think about what she should do, and tell herself "Don't hit. Do something better." Play stop and freeze games that help her learn to control impulses. If she learns to stop and freeze when you call her name, you can get to her and coach her through upsetting situations. It may also help to teach her to take a few deep breaths to relax. Be sure that this child has opportunities to see others solve problems without aggression. Demonstrate and comment on examples of cooperation that take place around her. Encourage children to work cooperatively by saying, "How can you work together to build that tower?" If it is necessary for this child to leave an upsetting activity, require her to choose a quiet activity by herself for a time. When she is in control of her emotions, she can rejoin the others. You will

Carrie ran across her living room as the fists began to fly. By the time she got to the girls, both Amy and Marie were frantic. Carrie took them by the hand and moved to the side of the room. Marie was sobbing, unable to stop. Both girls looked really scared.

Carrie thought she first needed to help the girls calm down. Carrie said to Amy, "Tell me what happened." Amy couldn't explain much except, "Marie kept hitting me." It appeared Amy no longer knew what had happened or else she couldn't put it into words. While still holding the hands of each girl, Carrie turned her attention to Marie. Marie was still crying but not as uncontrollably. She asked if Marie was hurt, but she shook her head no. Carrie asked Marie to tell her what had happened. Her response was much like Amy's, saying, "Amy was fighting me."

Carrie decided whatever had brought on the dispute had been lost in the emotions of the situation. Both children were still breathing hard and Carrie thought it was important for them to continue to relax. She asked the girls to choose between playdough or coloring. Amy chose playdough and Marie slunk down in a chair by the coloring materials. Before long, Amy had cooled off and could rejoin the group of players. It took a little longer and a little more support before Marie regained her composure. Carrie sat near her and colored a picture too. Occasionally, Carrie commented on her own picture. Eventually Marie joined the conversation.

probably need to assist with this reunion in order for it to be successful.

Work with the Parent(s)

Let the parent(s) know early on that there is a problem with the amount of aggressive behavior. Most parents will do all they can to decrease it. However, some parents may not know how to curb it or may have different feelings about how children should respond to conflict. It is not productive to blame the parent(s) for the child's aggression. Instead, let the parent(s) know that in your setting you will need to help their child learn other responses. Tell them it is your job to keep children safe, including keeping children from hitting or kicking one another. Ask for the parent's assistance in making sure that their child is well rested, has adequate exercise, and is well fed so that she arrives at your setting ready to face the daily challenges. Talk with the parent(s) about additional steps to take, using the Plan for Action.

When to Get Help

Learn more about working with a child who is aggressive by taking a class, attending a workshop, or reading one of the suggested resources. If you do not see a decrease in aggressive behaviors after trying these suggestions for a number of weeks, have an early childhood consultant observe and give suggestions specific to your situation.

If this child is having difficulty understanding social situations, the intricacies of pretend play, or if her language is lagging in development, have this child's skills screened to see if they are developing at an age-appropriate rate. If this child's skills are adequate but she is still aggressive many times per day after three to six months, recommend that the parent(s) contact a family counselor to help teach more effective coping skills.

For Further Reading

Crary, Elizabeth. *Children's Problem Solving Series*. Seattle: Parenting Press, 1982–1986.

———. *Kids Can Cooperate*. Seattle: Parenting Press, 1984.

Essa, Eva. *A Practical Guide to Solving Preschool Behavior Problems*. Albany, NY: Delmar Publishers, 1990.

Oken-Wright, Pam. "From Tug of War to 'Let's Make a Deal': The Teacher's Role." *Young Children* 48(1992): 15–20.

Our child care provider told us that Courtney hits other kids when she's upset. I don't know what to do about it. She's never hit anyone at home.

What Is It?

Aggressive behaviors cause a great deal of disruption and concern for both providers and parents. Typically, aggressive behaviors are those that injure people or property. Hitting, kicking, slapping, pulling hair, pinching, scratching, and biting are all aggressive behaviors. Biting seems to be extremely upsetting to those involved and is discussed separately in chapter 16, "Chomp! Biting."

Unfortunately, aggressive behavior can be a common problem with young children because they have not yet learned to express their strong emotions in more appropriate ways. When children come together in group settings, they are more likely to experience frustration and conflict that can cause aggression. Occasionally, children will demonstrate aggressive behaviors in a group setting but not at home. More typically, children use these behaviors in response to frustration in any setting.

Observe and Problem Solve

Knowing that aggression can be common doesn't make it easier to deal with. Observe the situations in which your child is aggressive. The following questions and suggestions will help as you formulate your plans.

➤ *Is your child trying to make contact with someone in an inappropriate manner? Is she trying to be friendly?*

Teach ways to touch that do not involve pushing or shoving. Children can shake hands and rub or pat their friend's back. Notice when your child is being friendly and using a gentle touch. Help her learn to greet another child or ask to play by offering an appealing play idea. (For more information on initiating play with others see chapter 11, "I Want to Play Too: Joining a Group of Players.")

➤ *Was a behavior misinterpreted and thought to be aggressive?*

When your child has friends over or is playing with brothers or sisters, be sure that there is enough room for play. Accidents are sometimes interpreted as aggression. Further aggression follows when the second child retaliates. You may need to quickly describe the situation as accidental. Say something like, "Sarah accidentally knocked down your blocks when she tried to get to her building. If you build farther over here it may not happen."

A child's actions might also be misinterpreted as they try to make room for themselves on the couch. Respond by saying something like, "Roshaan pushed you over because he wants to sit next to you." Consider if your child has difficulty understanding other aspects of play. A child who does not catch on to social feedback or does not comprehend complicated pretend play may become frustrated and strike out.

➤ *How much language is your child using?*

A child who uses very few words or who is difficult to understand is more likely to respond to a conflict with aggressive behaviors. You can help her learn words to use in difficult situations, come and get you for help, or even yell rather than hit. Once you are aware of the conflict, you can help by offering words she can use. Keep these words very simple. "Stop," "That's mine," or "Help" are examples. When your child is ready, teach more complex statements like "I was using that" or "When can I have a turn?" or "I want to play my ideas." Give her lots of positive attention for using words instead of hitting. If you can catch her before she is aggressive, tell her gently but firmly that she needs to use words.

➤ *Is she trying to engage another in roly-poly play? Has roly-poly play turned aggressive?*

Many children love to roll around and be physical as they play with others. To help meet this need, provide many indoor and outdoor movement opportunities each day. Consider having a time when you and your child can safely roughhouse. Set limits, including we both need to be ready to wrestle, stop when someone says "stop," and only wrestling. Help her get involved in another activity afterward. Adults can walk away from this type of play but children need help changing gears. Try sensory experiences such as playdough, time in the bath for water play, or fingerpainting with shaving cream. Give your child opportunities to be powerful in other ways by having her help to make rules, run errands, plan activities, and make choices. Comment on times when she uses "her strong muscles" to help rearrange furniture or climb to the top of playground equipment.

➤ *Is your child using aggression to express anger or to get what she wants?*

Teach your child to express anger in non-aggressive ways. Safe ways to express anger include telling someone, yelling, stamping feet, pounding playdough, or scribbling on a piece of paper. Model the use of words to express your own feelings of anger.

Be clear that aggression will not be permitted. Say, "I won't let you hit. Hitting hurts." You may need to direct your children through conflict situations by saying, "Troy was using that. You need to give the toy back. Ask him to give it to you when he is done with it." Older preschool children can begin to learn problem-solving skills. Help them to identify the problem, brainstorm solutions, pick one to try, and evaluate how it worked. Problem-solving meetings can help everyone calm down. Ask each child what happened. Then start problem solving by asking, "What can you do that will make both of you happy?" If they are unable to come up with any solutions, suggest a few for them.

➤ *Is your child hitting many times per day or for a number of months?*

If your child has persistent difficulty controlling her aggression, a concerted effort to reduce this behavior may be needed. Teach your child to recognize when she is angry, stop and think about what she should do, and tell herself "Don't hit. Do something better." Supervise closely so you can coach her through upsetting situations. It may also help to teach her to take a few deep breaths to relax.

If she is unable to work out her problem without hitting, she may need to leave an upset-

ting activity and choose a quiet activity to do by herself for a time. When she is in control of her emotions, she can rejoin you. Be sure to recognize and comment on times when she solves problems without aggression.

Reduce the number of aggressive models to which your child is exposed. If she watches a lot of television in which violence is portrayed, cut back on the amount she views. If her play is especially aggressive when playing about superheroes, you may need to limit the amount of time spent in this play or ask that it take place only outside. (For further information on this type of play, see the suggestions in chapter 10, "Let's Say I'm Batman: Superhero Play.") Be sure that your child has an opportunity to see others solve problems without aggression. Demonstrate and comment on examples of cooperation that take place around her.

Work with Your Provider

If you have not seen your child use aggression, you may be quite surprised to find out that she is using it in a group setting. Children can sometimes behave differently when they are with a group of same aged children than when they are at home with parents and siblings. Chances are, however, that you see similar behaviors at home. You can support your child and provider by talking with your provider about the steps you will take. Understand what an upsetting behavior this is when you are responsible for the safety of a number of children. You and your provider will want to reduce and/or eliminate aggressive behaviors as soon as possible. Use these suggestions and formulate a Plan for Action. Establish consistency between home and the early childhood setting to help your child learn appropriate behaviors more quickly. In addition, make sure that your child is well rested, has plenty of exercise and is well fed so she is ready to face the challenges of a group situation.

When to Get Help

Learn more about reducing aggression by taking a class, attending a workshop, or reading one of the suggested resources. If your child is having difficulty understanding social situations and the intricacies of pretend play, or if her language is lagging in development, have her skills screened to see if they are developing at an age-appropriate rate. If your child is still aggressive many times per day after three to six months, contact a parent educator or counselor for help in teaching more effective coping skills.

For Further Reading

Crary, Elizabeth. *Children's Problem Solving Series*. Seattle: Parenting Press, 1982–1986.

———. *Kids Can Cooperate*. Seattle: Parenting Press, 1984.

Essa, Eva. *A Practical Guide to Solving Preschool Behavior Problems*. Albany, NY: Delmar Publishers, 1990.

A Plan for Action

To develop your Plan for Action, choose a goal that best fits your situation. Then determine three or four actions providers and parent(s) will take. Choose additional actions specific to the early childhood setting and home. Mark your choices on this summary or write them on the planning form that follows.

Sample goals for a child who is aggressive:
- Uses gentle touch in approaching others.
- Keeps hands to self when close to other children.
- Engages in roly-poly play at appropriate times and in appropriate spaces.
- Expresses anger without aggression.
- Brings problems to an adult for help in solving.
- Actively helps in problem solving.
- Problem solves independently.
- Add your ideas.

Sample actions parent(s) and provider can take:
- Teach gentle touch.
- Teach ways to greet others.
- Provide sensory activities.
- Provide indoor and outdoor movement opportunities.
- Make sure there is adequate space for an activity.
- Give opportunities for this child to be powerful.
- Be clear that aggression will not be permitted.
- Teach safe ways to express anger.
- Help this child recognize angry feelings and to stop and think.
- Teach words to use when upset and to express wants and feelings.
- Teach problem solving.
- Label accidental situations.
- Add your ideas.

Sample actions provider can take:
- Define personal space.
- Teach this child and others to say "move over please."
- Separate those who are having difficulty sitting next to one another.
- Play stop-and-freeze games to teach control.
- Ask that this child choose a quiet activity to do by herself when she needs to calm down.
- Assist this child in joining other children.
- Provide a space where it is okay to wrestle.
- Learn more about working with aggressive behaviors. Share pertinent information with parent(s).
- Have an early childhood consultant in to observe your interactions. Share pertinent information with parent(s).
- Add your ideas.

Sample actions parent(s) can take:
- Comment on examples of cooperation.
- Comment on times when this child solves problems without aggression.
- Set limits on roughhousing.
- Encourage play that is not only about superheroes.
- Reduce the amount of aggressive television this child views.
- Arrange for a developmental screening to be done by your health care provider or the early childhood assessment program in your school district. Share pertinent information with your provider.
- Talk with a parent educator or counselor. Share pertinent information with your provider.
- Add your ideas.

Parent(s) and Provider Action Form

Date:_____

Our plan for _____
          (CHILD'S NAME)

Goal

Write a realistic goal for this child using one of the examples from this chapter or one of your own.

_____
_____
_____
_____

Actions parent(s) and provider will take

Choose from those in this chapter or use your own ideas.

1. _____
2. _____
3. _____
4. _____

Actions provider will take

Choose from those in this chapter or use your own ideas.

1. _____
2. _____

Actions parent(s) will take

Choose from those in this chapter or use your own ideas.

1. _____
2. _____

We will check in to discuss progress or modify our plan on_____

(set a day six weeks to three months from now).

Signed

_____

(provider)

_____

(parent)

CHAPTER 16

Chomp!
Biting

I turned my back for just a second and one of the children started screaming. I knew right away what had happened—Nathan was biting again.

What Is It?

Biting is an upsetting behavior that can result from feelings of frustration, overstimulation, anger, hunger, and pain related to teething. Often, children use biting as a way to get their needs met because they do not have more appropriate methods of communicating what they want and because biting gets a strong response from others. Whatever the reason for biting, this behavior evokes strong emotions from all those involved, including the child who bites, the "victim," the parents of both children, and the provider. When the injury breaks the skin, it may require medical attention. Unfortunately, biting often takes place when a number of young children come together.

Observe and Problem Solve

The first step in dealing with biting is to take a few deep breaths and try to make sure that you are calm. Then help all the children feel calm before doing anything about the situation. Ask the following questions as you try to learn about what is taking place. When you can answer the questions below, the solutions may become clearer.

➤ *When does this child bite?*

If there is any pattern to the time the biting takes place, you may be able to rearrange your schedule to better meet the child's needs. For instance, try adding a rest period or special activity during the times when biting often occurs. Spend a few minutes early each day giving this child plenty of attention when he is not biting.

➤ *Could this child be hungry?*

Some children fall apart behaviorally when they are hungry. Give this child a snack before he reaches this point or change mealtimes so that he eats a little earlier.

➤ *Does this child seem frustrated?*

Reduce this child's frustration level by making activities easier for him. Sometimes children are frustrated because they feel crowded. Find ways for this child to have more space in which to work or play. Break the large group into smaller groups a few times each day. You may find that this child is frustrated because others are trying to take his materials or because there is a toy he wants and he is not getting a turn. Cut down on this type of frustration by adding duplicates of favorite toys whenever possible.

➤ *Does this child bite when there is less adult supervision?*

Usually, biting takes place during times that children are playing independent of adults. For the next few months, you may need to spend a lot of individual time with this child during free play periods. When he has had adequate attention, he may not resort to biting as often. Try adding more structured activities and reduce the amount of free play for a few weeks. Calming activities such as water play or playdough may be helpful when it is not possible to closely supervise.

➤ *Does this child bite one person in particular?*

Sometimes a child acts with aggression toward a particular child. If so, you may need to separate these two whenever you are not able to play along with them. If, however, this child resorts to biting anyone, protect the other children by keeping the one who is biting with you at all times.

➤ *How much language is the child using?*

A child who uses very few words or who is difficult to understand is more likely to respond to a conflict with aggressive behavior. You can help him to learn words to use in difficult situations, get you for help, or even yell rather than bite. Once you are aware of the conflict, you can help by offering words he can use. Keep these words very simple. "Stop," "That's mine," or "Help" are examples. Give him lots of positive reinforcement for using words instead of biting. If you can catch him before he bites, tell him gently but firmly that he needs to use words.

Don't bite the child back or use aggression to try to change the child's behavior. If an adult bites or hits the child in response to his biting, these actions teach that it is okay to bite or hit if you are bigger or stronger. Instead, teach the child new behaviors that will help him handle his frustrations.

If you must remove this child from an upsetting activity for a short time, ask him to choose a quiet activity to do by himself. When he has calmed down, he can rejoin the others. You will probably need to assist in this reunion in order for it to be successful.

➤ *How many times each day is the child biting?*

Because this behavior is so disturbing, it can sometimes seem as though it happens all the time. Watch to see how often the child is biting, and then compare this number to the number of times another child of the same age is aggressive. You may find that there isn't a big difference. Recognizing this can help you gain perspective. Knowing the actual number of incidents will also be helpful when you discuss the problem with the parent(s) of the child who is biting. After implementing your Plan for Action, count the number of incidents again to see the growth and improvement.

Work with the Parent(s)

Talk with the parent(s) of the child who is biting about the situation. Be aware that they may have never seen the child bite. This is often true when the child is an only child or has rarely been in a group setting with the parent(s). Inform them about what is taking place. Reassure them that you are doing everything possible to keep the child from biting. Ask them if they are experiencing any biting at home. Give them the information on biting for parents and ask them to meet with you to develop a Plan for Action. Consistency between home and the early childhood setting will help this child learn appropriate behaviors more quickly.

The parents of other children may want to know who is doing the biting. The children may tell them. Be sure you keep specific information about the problem confidential. Reassure them that you are doing what you can to help the child learn not to bite and to keep their child safe.

When to Get Help

Biting can be common between the ages of fourteen and twenty-four months and for some young preschool children who are not yet very verbal. When a preschool-aged child bites, it can be an especially difficult behavior to work with. Get help early in the development of the problem. For additional information on aggressive behavior, see the suggested resources as well as chapter 15, "Whack! Aggression." Talk with your director or a mentor about your feelings and possible solutions. If the behavior occurs daily or persists over several months despite your efforts to prevent it, talk with a consultant who will be able to give suggestions specific to your situation. Check the child's language development by suggesting the parent(s) have this child's language skills screened. If needed, suggest they talk with a parent educator or a counselor who specializes in working with young children.

For Further Reading

Crary, Elizabeth. *Without Spanking or Spoiling.* Seattle: Parenting Press, 1993.

Essa, Eva. *A Practical Guide to Solving Preschool Behavior Problems.* Albany, NY: Delmar Publishers, 1990.

We were playing hide-and-seek under a blanket and all of a sudden Nathan gave me a Dracula chomp right on my forearm. I was so surprised I didn't know what to do.

What Is It?

Biting is an upsetting behavior that can result from feelings of frustration, overstimulation, anger, hunger, and pain related to teething. Often, children use biting as a way to get their needs met because they do not yet have more appropriate methods of communicating what they want and because biting gets a strong response from others. Whatever the reason for biting, this behavior evokes strong emotions from all those involved, including the child who bites, the "victim," the parents of both children, and the provider.

Observe and Problem Solve

The first step in dealing with biting is to take a few deep breaths and try to make sure that you are calm. Then help your child feel calm before doing anything about the situation. Ask the following questions as you try to learn about what is taking place. When you can answer the questions below, the solutions may become clearer.

➤ *When does your child bite?*

If there is any pattern to the time the biting takes place, you may be able to rearrange your schedule to better meet your child's needs. For example, if the biting seems to take place on a Monday after a busy weekend or when his schedule has been disrupted, you might need to stick closer to routine and make sure he is well rested. Spend a few minutes each day cuddling before dropping him off at your early childhood program. If biting occurs only when he is in a group setting, you may not be able to do much to help during the "heat of the moment." However, you can support your provider by using some of the suggestions that follow.

➤ *Could your child be hungry?*

Some children fall apart behaviorally when they are hungry. Give him a snack before he reaches this point or change mealtimes so that he eats a little earlier. Make sure he has a big breakfast before going to his early childhood program or supply an extra snack if needed.

➤ *Does your child seem frustrated?*

Reduce the child's frustration level by making activities easier for him. Sometimes children are frustrated because they feel crowded. Find ways to give him more space.

➤ *Does your child seem too excited?*

Watch to see what signals your child gives as he is becoming overstimulated. Does his face become flushed, voice grow louder, or breathing become more rapid? Recognize the signals and stop an exciting activity before he reaches the point of biting.

➤ *How much language is your child using?*

A child who uses very few words or who is difficult to understand is more likely to respond to a conflict with aggressive behaviors. You can help him to learn words to use in difficult situations, get you for help, or even yell rather than bite. Once you are aware of the conflict, you can help by offering words he can use. Keep these words very simple. "Stop," "That's mine," or "Help" are examples. Give him lots of positive attention for using words instead of biting. If you can catch him before he bites, tell him gently but firmly that he needs to use words.

Don't bite your child back or use aggression to try to change the child's behavior. If an adult bites or hits the child in response to his biting, these actions teach that it is okay to bite or hit if you are bigger or stronger. Instead, teach your child new behaviors that will help him handle his frustrations.

If you must remove your child from an upsetting activity for a short time, ask him to choose a quiet activity to do by himself. When he has calmed down, he can rejoin the others. You will probably need to assist in this reunion in order for it to be successful.

➤ *Does your child bite siblings or you?*

Sometimes children will be aggressive toward younger brothers or sisters because they feel jealous or do not know how to express their anger. If so, you may need to protect younger children by keeping one of the two with you whenever possible. If your child is biting older brothers or sisters, it may be that he is feeling powerless. Your child may be frustrated because others are trying to take his materials or because there is a toy he wants and he isn't getting a turn. Teach both children ways to talk about what they want and ways to negotiate what they will do together. Some children bite anyone that is in their way, even their parents. Talk with your child about gentle touch. Be sure you make it clear to your child that biting hurts and that you will not allow this behavior. If you have been holding your child, put him down and say, "Biting hurts. I don't like it when you bite me." Withhold your attention for a short time. Then give him a chance to try again. Get him started in a more appropriate activity.

➤ *How often is your child biting?*

Consider how often your child is biting and if the behavior has taken place for a number of months. You will also need to find out how often the behavior is taking place in your early childhood program. Ask your provider to help you record the incidents. When you know how often the behavior is taking place, you can get a better perspective on the severity of the problem. This figure will also help you recognize the growth and improvement made as the number of incidents decrease.

Work with Your Provider

Whether or not your child bites frequently or you see it at home, you and your provider will want to work together to eliminate the biting and teach new skills as soon as possible. A consistent approach at home and in your early childhood setting will help your child get the message that this is not acceptable behavior. In most cases, biting will decrease when adults focus on preventing frustration and teaching words to use to express feelings and solve problems.

When to Get Help

Biting can be common between the ages of fourteen and twenty-four months and for some young preschool children who are not yet very verbal. When a preschool-aged child bites, it can be especially difficult. For additional information on aggressive behaviors, see the suggested resources as well as chapter 15, "Whack! Aggression." If your child is biting daily or for a period of several months, have a speech and language specialist or the early childhood assessment program in your school district screen his language skills. If needed, contact a parent educator or a counselor who specializes in working with young children.

For Further Reading

Crary, Elizabeth. *Without Spanking or Spoiling.* Seattle: Parenting Press, 1993.

Essa, Eva. *A Practical Guide to Solving Preschool Behavior Problems.* Albany, NY: Delmar Publishers, 1990.

A Plan for Action

To develop your Plan for Action, choose a goal that best fits your situation. Then determine three or four actions providers and parent(s) will take. Choose additional actions specific to the early childhood setting and home. Mark your choices on this summary or write them on the planning form that follows.

Sample goals for a child who bites:
- Uses gentle touch in approaching others.
- Gets an adult to help when he is frustrated.
- Uses words when upset or angry.
- Brings problems to an adult for help in problem solving.
- Actively helps in problem solving.
- Problem solves independently.
- Add your ideas.

Sample actions parent(s) and provider can take:
- Offer activity choices that are at this child's developmental level.
- Teach gentle touch.
- Stop activities that are too exciting before this child bites.
- Teach words to use when this child is frustrated.
- Respond to biting incidents by telling this child "biting hurts."
- Help this child get started in a more appropriate activity.
- Add your ideas.

Sample actions provider can take:
- Make sure this child has plenty of room to work and play.
- Arrange a rest time when this child tires.
- Schedule snack or meals earlier if this child is hungry.
- Get more of the favorite toys and materials.
- Spend time one-on-one with this child early in the day.
- Keep this child busy with adult-directed activities.
- Offer calming activities.
- Break the large group into smaller groups a few times each day.
- Separate this child from a child he is biting as much as possible.
- Arrange for an adult to supervise this child closely throughout the day.
- Learn more about ways to work with a child who bites. Share pertinent information with the parent(s).
- Talk with an early childhood consultant. Share pertinent information with the parent(s).
- Add your ideas.

Sample actions parent(s) can take:
- Make sure your child is well rested.
- Offer your child a big meal before drop off.
- Bring an extra snack for this child each day.
- Spend some time cuddling each day before drop off.
- Arrange for a speech and language screening. Share pertinent information with your provider.
- Talk with a parent educator or counselor. Share pertinent information with your provider.
- Add your ideas.

This chapter has used information from *What's Appropriate,* Helpline brochure #7, made possible through a joint venture of Greater Minneapolis Day Care Association and Resources for Child Caring, Inc., with funds from the McKnight Foundation.

Parent(s) and Provider Action Form

Date:_____

Our plan for _____
             (CHILD'S NAME)

Goal

Write a realistic goal for this child using one of the examples from this chapter or one of your own.

_____
_____
_____
_____

Actions parent(s) and provider will take

Choose from those in this chapter or use your own ideas.

1. _____
2. _____
3. _____
4. _____

Actions provider will take

Choose from those in this chapter or use your own ideas.

1. _____
2. _____

Actions parent(s) will take

Choose from those in this chapter or use your own ideas.

1. _____
2. _____

We will check in to discuss progress or modify our plan on_____
(set a day six weeks to three months from now).

Signed

_____
(provider)

_____
(parent)

Bibliography

Anoka-Hennepin Community Education Learning Readiness/Preschool. *Large Muscle Curriculum*. Edited by Debbie Hewitt. Anoka, MN: unpublished, 1994.

Beaty, Janice J. *Observing the Development of the Young Child*. Columbus, OH: Charles E. Merrill Publishing Company, 1994.

Beebe, Brooke McKamy. *Tips for Toddlers*. New York: Dell Publishing, 1983.

Berman, Christine, and Jacki Fromer. *Meals Without Squeals*. Palo Alto, CA: Bull Publishing, 1991.

Brazelton, T. Berry. *Working and Caring*. Reading, MA: Addison-Wesley Publishing, 1985.

Brenner, Barbara. *The Preschool Handbook*. New York: Pantheon Books, 1990.

Brick, Peggy, Sue Montfort, and Nancy Blume. *Healthy Foundations: The Teacher's Book*. Hackensack, NJ: The Center for Family Life Education, 1993.

Budd, Linda. *Living With the Active Alert Child*. Seattle: Parenting Press, 1993.

Carlsson-Paige, Nancy, and Diane Levin. *Who's Calling the Shots?* Philadelphia: New Society Publishing, 1990.

Cherry, Clare. *Think of Something Quiet*. Carthage, IL: Fearon Teacher Aids, 1981.

Crary, Elizabeth. *Children's Problem Solving Series*. Seattle: Parenting Press, 1982-1986.

———. *Kids Can Cooperate*. Seattle: Parenting Press, 1984.

———. *Without Spanking or Spoiling*. Seattle: Parenting Press, 1993.

Curry, Nancy, and Carl Johnson. *Beyond Self Esteem: Developing a Genuine Sense of Human Value*. Washington DC: NAEYC, 1990.

Ekman, Paul. *Why Kids Lie*. New York: Charles Scribner's Sons, 1989.

Essa, Eva. *A Practical Guide to Solving Preschool Behavior Problems*. Albany, NY: Delmar Publishers, 1990.

Eyre, Linda, and Richard Eyre. *Teaching Your Children Values*. New York: Simon & Schuster, 1993.

Faber, Adele, and Elaine Mazlish. *How to Talk So Kids Will Listen and Listen So Kids Will Talk*. New York: Avon Books, 1980.

Fry-Miller, Kathleen, and Judith Myers-Wells. *Young Peacemakers Project Book*. Elgin. IL: Brethren Press, 1988.

Galinsky, Ellen, and Judy David. *The Preschool Years*. New York: Times Books, 1988.

Garber, Stephen, Marianne Garber, and Robyn Spizman. *Monsters Under the Bed and Other Childhood Fears*. New York: Villard Books, 1993.

Gartrell, Daniel. *A Guidance Approach to Discipline*. Albany, NY: Delmar Publishers, 1994.

———. "Punishment or Guidance?" *Young Children* 42(1987): 55–61.

Goldstein, Robin. *More Everyday Parenting*. New York: Penguin Books, 1991.

Greenberg, Polly. *Character Development: Encouraging Self-Esteem & Self Discipline in Infants, Toddlers, & Two-Year-Olds*. Washington, DC: NAEYC, 1991.

Greenspan, Nancy, and Stanley Greenspan. *The Essential Partnership: How Parents and Children Can Meet the Emotional Challenges of Infancy and Childhood*. New York: Viking, 1989.

Greenspan, Stanley. *Playground Politics*. Reading, MA: Addison-Wesley Publishing, 1993.

Grisanti, Mary Lee, Dian Smith, and Charles Flatter. *Parents' Guide to Understanding Discipline Infancy through Preteen*. New York: Prentice Hall Press, 1990.

Hazen, Nancy, Betty Black, and Faye Fleming-Johnson. "Social Acceptance." *Young Children* 39(1984): 26–36.

Heidemann, Sandra, and Deborah Hewitt. *Pathways to Play*. St. Paul: Redleaf Press, 1992.

Hewitt, Debbie. "Dragon Play and Other Drama." *Family Day Caring*. March/April (1992): 6–7.

———. "They Said I Can't Play." *Family Day Caring*. September/October (1992): 6-7.

Hi-Tops Video. *Baby Songs*. Distributed by Video Treasures, 2001 Glenn Parkway, Batavia, Ohio 45103, 1989.

Howarth, Mary. "Rediscovering the Power of Fairy Tales." *Young Children* 45(1989): 58-65.

Johnson, Dorothy Davies. *I Can't Sit Still*. Santa Cruz, CA: ETR Associates, 1992.

Katz, Lilian. "The Professional Early Childhood Teacher." *Young Children* 39(1984): 3–10.

Kitzinger, Sheila, and Celia Kitzinger. *Tough Questions*. Boston: The Harvard Common Press, 1991.

Kurcinka, Mary Sheedy. *Raising Your Spirited Child*. New York: Harper Perennial, 1991.

Lansky, Vicki. *Toilet Training*. Toronto: Bantam Books, 1984.

Leight, L. *Raising Sexually Healthy Children*. New York: Rawson Associates, 1988.

Mack, Allison. *Toilet Learning*. Boston: Little Brown & Company, 1978.

Marion, Marian. *Guidance of Young Children*. Columbus: Merrill Publishing, 1991.

McCarney, Stephen, and Angela Bauer. *The Parent's Guide*. Columbia, MO: Hawthorne Educational Services, 1989.

Oken-Wright, Pam. "From Tug of War to 'Let's Make a Deal': The Teacher's Role." *Young Children* 48(1992): 15–20.

Oppenheim, Joanne, Betty Boegehold, and Barbara Brenner. *Raising a Confident Child*. New York: Pantheon Books, 1984.

Park, Mary Joan. *Peacemaking for Little Friends*. St. Paul: Little Friends for Peace, 1985.

Philadelphia Child Guidance Center. *Your Child's Emotional Health*. New York: Macmillan Publishing, 1993.

Piaget, Jean. *The Moral Judgment of the Child*. New York: The Free Press, 1965.

Provider's Choice, Inc. *The Shape of Good Nutrition*. Minneapolis: Provider's Choice, 1994.

Ramsey, Patricia. *Making Friends in School*. New York: Teachers College Press, 1991.

Rubin, Douglas. *Bratbusters*. El Paso, TX: Skidmore-Roth Publishing, 1992.

Rubin, Richard, John Fisher, and Susan Doering. *Your Toddler*. New York: Macmillan Publishing, 1980.

Saifer, Steffen. *Practical Solutions to Practically Every Problem*. St. Paul: Redleaf Press, 1990.

Satter, Ellyn. *How to Get Your Kid to Eat . . . But Not Too Much*. Palo Alto, CA: Bull Publishing, 1987.

Sobel, Jeffrey. *Everybody Wins: 393 Non-Competitive Games for Young Children*. New York: Walker and Company, 1983.

Torbert, Marianne, and Lynne Schneider. *Follow Me Too*. Reading, MA: Addison-Wesley Publishing Company, 1993.

Turecki, Stanley. *The Difficult Child*. New York: Bantam Books, 1985.

Wallach, Lorraine. "Helping Children Cope with Violence." *Young Children*. 48, no. 4 (1993): 4–11.

Wilson, Pamela. *When Sex Is the Subject*. Santa Cruz, CA: Network Publications, 1991.

Wycoff, Jerry, and Barbara Unell. *Discipline Without Shouting or Spanking*. New York: Meadowbrook Press, 1984.

About the Author

Deborah Hewitt began her work with young children as a therapeutic preschool teacher in the inner city. She has gone on to consult with child care providers, serve as a CDA Advisor, provide workshops for early childhood educators, serve on the board of directors of MnA-EYC, and now is a trainer-of-trainers. Along with these roles, she continues her work with children teaching in a Learning Readiness preschool program.

In 1992, Deborah and a colleague published *Pathways to Play*, which provides suggestions for promoting young children's play and social skills. Deborah has also written training curriculums on guiding behavior and child development. Articles she has written have appeared in *Family Day Caring*, a national publication.

Deborah lives with her husband and their two children in Minneapolis, Minnesota. Her experiences parenting, providing care for children in early childhood programs, and as a consumer of child care services have contributed to her understanding of guidance and parent-provider communication. Her commitment to promoting high quality care for young children drives all aspects of her work.

Also From Redleaf Press

The Kindness Curriculum: Introducing Young Children to Loving Values - Over 60 imaginative, exuberant activities that create opportunities for kids to practice kindness, empathy, conflict resolution, respect, and more.

Making It Better: Activities for Children Living in a Stressful World - Bold, new information about the physical and emotional effects of stress, trauma, and violence on children today. Help children survive, thrive, and learn.

Open the Door Let's Explore More! Field Trips of Discovery for Young Children - Revised and expanded, this new edition of the popular *Open the Door Let's Explore* is filled with activities to do before, during, and after field trips to reinforce learning while having fun.

Prime Times: A Handbook for Excellence in Infant and Toddler Programs - Learn how to organize and implement a program of excellent care and education for infants and toddlers, how to staff a program, and how to establish and keep quality caregiving vital.

Reflecting Children's Lives: A Handbook for Planning Child-Centered Curriculum - A practical guide to help you put children and childhood at the center of your curriculum. Rethink and refresh your ideas about scheduling, observations, play, materials, space, and emergent themes.

Roots and Wings: Affirming Culture in Early Childhood Programs - A unique approach to multicultural education that helps shape positive attitudes toward cultural difference.

Training Teachers: A Harvest of Theory and Practice - A creative synthesis of some of the best ideas in teaching and learning put into action with innovative training tools and new strategies.

Transition Magician: Strategies for Guiding Young Children in Early Childhood Programs - Over 200 original, fun activities that help you magically turn transition time into calm, smooth activity changes.

For more information or a free full-color catalog featuring these and other titles call

**Redleaf Press
800-423-8309**